Magnetism: The Art Of Attracting Anyone Effortlessly

Jason Lorayne

Published by Akashic Records, 2024.

While every precaution has been taken in the preparation of this book, the publisher assumes no responsibility for errors or omissions, or for damages resulting from the use of the information contained herein.

MAGNETISM: THE ART OF ATTRACTING ANYONE EFFORTLESSLY

First edition. November 6, 2024.

Copyright © 2024 Jason Lorayne.

ISBN: 979-8227654595

Written by Jason Lorayne.

Introduction: The Power of Attraction

Attraction is an intricate dance, an invisible thread that connects us to certain individuals, igniting a spark that can lead to profound relationships or fleeting moments. As someone who has spent years exploring the nuances of love, romance, and psychology, I've come to understand that attraction is far more complex than mere physical appeal. It's an interplay of biology, psychology, and environment that shapes our connections.

Understanding Attraction: The Psychology Behind Why We Are Drawn to Certain People

Attraction begins at a fundamental level with biological instincts. Our brains are wired to seek out traits that signal health, genetic compatibility, and social status. Research indicates that certain characteristics—such as facial symmetry, clear skin, and even specific scents—can trigger attraction on a subconscious level. These signals often originate from our evolutionary past, where our ancestors relied on such traits to choose suitable mates. For instance, a study published in the *Journal of Personality and Social*

Psychology found that people consistently rated faces with symmetrical features as more attractive. This pattern speaks to an innate preference for what signifies health and genetic fitness.

But while biology sets the stage, psychology plays an equally crucial role in determining whom we find attractive. The concept of proximity, for instance, suggests that the more we encounter someone, the more likely we are to develop feelings for them. This phenomenon is known as the mere exposure effect. It's why we often find ourselves attracted to colleagues or classmates, even if they don't fit our usual "type." Being around someone repeatedly allows us to build familiarity, which can breed comfort and affection.

Emotional connections also enhance attraction. Research shows that shared experiences, particularly those that evoke strong emotions, can deepen our bond with someone. Engaging in activities that spark joy or excitement—whether it's hiking, attending a concert, or even tackling a challenging project—can create a shared emotional history that strengthens attraction. When we navigate challenges together or celebrate victories, we form a unique connection that elevates our feelings for one another.

Another critical factor is the impact of self-esteem on attraction. Individuals with higher self-esteem often project confidence, making them more appealing to others. This isn't merely about looking good; it's about how we carry ourselves and engage with the world. People are drawn to those who exude positivity and self-assuredness. Practicing self-love and nurturing our own self-esteem can amplify our magnetic presence, making it easier to attract others.

Moreover, personality traits play a significant role in attraction. Traits such as kindness, humor, and emotional intelligence are consistently rated highly by those looking for a partner. A study published in *The Journal of Social Psychology* indicated that people are more attracted to those who display warmth and sociability. When we are approachable and empathetic, we foster an environment where others feel comfortable, which naturally draws them to us.

Additionally, the allure of mystery should not be overlooked. There's a fine line between being open and being an open book. Those who retain a sense of intrigue can pique interest, prompting others to want to learn more about them. This doesn't mean playing games or pretending to be someone you're not. Instead, it's about revealing layers of yourself gradually, allowing the other person to engage and invest in the discovery process.

While these psychological underpinnings of attraction offer valuable insights, it's essential to remember that attraction is not always straightforward. Personal preferences and unique experiences shape who we are drawn to, leading to a diverse array of attractions that can defy conventional wisdom. Understanding our motivations and the factors that drive our attractions can empower us in our relationships, allowing us to navigate the complexities of human connection with greater ease.

The Myth of the "Perfect" Person

The idea of the "perfect" person is one that has captivated hearts and minds for generations. Movies, books, and fairy tales often portray an idealized version of love, suggesting that a flawless partner exists just waiting to be discovered. Yet, the reality is far more nuanced. The myth of perfection can lead to unrealistic expectations that hinder genuine connections.

In my own journey, I have often encountered individuals who were obsessed with finding someone who met every criterion on their checklist. This quest for perfection often resulted in disappointment, as no one ever truly matched the ideal. This pursuit not only undermined potential relationships but also led to a cycle of dissatisfaction and loneliness. Research suggests that when we fixate on perfection, we may overlook the beauty of genuine connections that develop through vulnerability and shared experiences.

In reality, the qualities that foster deep, meaningful relationships are often found in our imperfections. A study in *Personality and Social Psychology Bulletin* revealed that people often find imperfections—whether they are quirks in personality or physical attributes—endearing. Embracing our own flaws and recognizing the imperfections in others can pave the way for authentic connections that are rich and fulfilling. The charm of a crooked smile or a laugh that comes too loud can create moments of intimacy that far outweigh any superficial ideal.

Furthermore, the notion of a "soulmate" can create a false dichotomy, leading many to believe that they must find one specific person destined to complete them. This can breed dependency and stifle personal growth. Instead of seeking someone to fill a void, it's far healthier to approach relationships with the mindset of companionship. Understanding that we can form meaningful bonds with multiple people throughout our lives opens us up to a wealth of experiences and connections that enrich our lives.

Additionally, the emphasis on compatibility can overshadow the importance of complementary differences. While shared values and interests are important, differences can spark growth and innovation in relationships. A study in *Psychological Science* found that couples who embrace their differences often report higher satisfaction levels than those who only focus on compatibility. This diversity can bring balance and depth to a relationship, making it all the more enriching.

Practical advice for those navigating the world of attraction includes fostering self-awareness. Reflecting on what you truly value in a partner—not just what society dictates—can guide you toward more fulfilling connections. Create a list of qualities that resonate with your core beliefs, but allow room for flexibility. Instead of seeking perfection, focus on finding someone whose strengths complement your own and whose weaknesses you can accept.

Another key strategy is to cultivate your own interests and passions. When you engage fully in your own life, you naturally become more attractive to others. Pursuing hobbies, joining clubs, or participating in community events can expand your social circle and introduce you to people who share your enthusiasm. When you are genuinely interested in your own life, it shines through and draws others in.

Moreover, practicing vulnerability is crucial in developing authentic relationships. Open up about your thoughts, fears, and dreams. Allow others to see the real you, imperfections and all. This vulnerability fosters trust and encourages deeper connections, allowing attraction to flourish organically. It's a delicate balance—showing enough of yourself to spark interest while keeping some mystery alive.

Ultimately, attraction is an art that requires understanding, patience, and a willingness to embrace the beauty of imperfection. By breaking free from the constraints of the "perfect" person myth and fostering a deeper awareness of ourselves and others, we can create meaningful connections that resonate with authenticity and joy. This journey through the complexities of attraction is not just about finding someone to love; it's about learning to love ourselves and the unique tapestry of human connection that surrounds us.

Chapter 1: The Foundations of Charisma
The Charismatic Mindset

Charisma often feels like an elusive quality reserved for the naturally gifted. Many people believe it's an innate trait that some possess and others lack. However, the truth is that charisma is less about an inherent personality type and more about cultivating a mindset that fosters confidence and self-assuredness. In my own experiences, I've witnessed how small shifts in mindset can significantly enhance one's magnetic presence. Research backs this up, revealing that charisma can be developed through intentional practice and self-awareness.

Understanding Charisma

At its core, charisma is a blend of confidence, warmth, and a compelling presence. Psychological studies reveal that people are naturally drawn to those who exude self-assurance, as it signals competence and reliability. A 2018 study published in the *Journal of Personality and Social Psychology* found that individuals perceived as confident were also rated as more likable and trustworthy. This underscores the idea that confidence not only attracts people but also fosters deeper connections.

To cultivate this confidence, it's essential to start from within. Self-assuredness begins with a positive self-image. Reflecting on my journey, I can attest to the transformative power of self-acceptance. Early in my career, I struggled with imposter syndrome, often doubting my abilities and feeling like a fraud. It was through persistent self-reflection and acknowledgment of my achievements—no matter how small—that I gradually built a more positive self-image.

One effective strategy for enhancing self-image is to engage in positive self-talk. The way we communicate with ourselves shapes our mindset and influences our external interactions. A study from *The*

University of California found that individuals who practiced positive affirmations reported higher levels of self-esteem and overall happiness. Creating a daily ritual of affirming your strengths can set a constructive tone for your day, reinforcing the belief that you have valuable contributions to make.

Additionally, setting achievable goals can foster a sense of accomplishment that bolsters confidence. Break larger ambitions into smaller, manageable tasks. Celebrate each success along the way, no matter how minor it may seem. This not only reinforces a sense of progress but also helps to create a positive feedback loop, where each small win builds on the last, creating a foundation of self-assuredness.

The Role of Body Language

While mindset is vital, nonverbal communication plays a critical role in how charisma is perceived. Research from *Harvard University* indicates that body language can significantly impact how others perceive our confidence levels. Adopting open, expansive postures—like standing tall with shoulders back—can signal confidence not only to others but also to ourselves. When we physically embody confidence, our mindset shifts accordingly.

In my experience, consciously practicing body language has been transformative. When I noticed how my posture affected my feelings of confidence, I began to incorporate power poses into my routine. Before important meetings or social interactions, I would take a moment to stand in a power pose—feet shoulder-width apart, hands on hips, and chest out. This simple act made a noticeable difference in how I felt and how I was received.

Mirroring is another effective technique for enhancing charisma. Subtly reflecting the body language of those around you can create a sense of rapport and connection. A study published in *Social Psychological and Personality Science* demonstrated that mirroring can enhance interpersonal attraction, making the other person feel understood and appreciated. This practice fosters a warm, inviting atmosphere that invites deeper engagement.

Cultivating Empathy and Connection

Charisma is not solely about projecting confidence; it's equally about connecting with others on a meaningful level. Cultivating empathy allows us to tune into the emotions of those around us, fostering an environment where people feel seen and valued. Research from *Emory University* highlights that empathy can enhance social bonding, leading to more profound connections and increased likability.

To enhance your empathetic skills, practice active listening. This involves not only hearing the words being spoken but also being attuned to the emotions behind them. When engaged in conversation, focus entirely on the speaker, avoiding distractions. Show genuine interest by asking open-ended questions that invite deeper exploration. This not only demonstrates empathy but also encourages the other person to share more, creating a richer dialogue.

Another powerful practice is to cultivate curiosity about others. Approach interactions with the mindset of wanting to learn from the person in front of you. This curiosity not only enriches your understanding of others but also positions you as someone who values connection over superficiality. People are drawn to those who make them feel important and interesting, enhancing your charismatic presence.

Embracing Vulnerability

A critical aspect of charisma is the willingness to be vulnerable. In a world that often prioritizes perfection and self-assurance, showing vulnerability can create powerful connections. Brené Brown's research on vulnerability reveals that it fosters trust and belonging, making others feel more comfortable in your presence.

In my own life, I found that sharing personal stories or experiences—even those that were challenging—invited others to relate to me on a deeper level. This openness not only humanizes us but also encourages others to share their own experiences, fostering an atmosphere of authenticity. Vulnerability can be a powerful tool for building relationships, as it breaks down barriers and creates a safe space for genuine connection.

To practice vulnerability, start small. Share a personal anecdote or a challenge you've faced in a conversation. Notice how this openness affects the dynamic of the interaction. You may find that others are more willing to reciprocate, leading to a more meaningful exchange.

Developing Presence and Mindfulness

Being present in the moment is a hallmark of charisma. When we engage fully with others, we create a magnetic presence that draws people in. Research from *Stanford University* suggests that mindfulness can enhance interpersonal relationships, as it allows us to be fully attuned to our surroundings and the people we interact with.

In my journey, mindfulness has become an essential practice. Regular meditation and mindfulness exercises have helped me cultivate a greater awareness of my thoughts and feelings. When I engage in conversations, I consciously remind myself to be present, letting go of distractions and focusing solely on the person in front of me. This practice not only enhances my interactions but also enriches my understanding of others.

To integrate mindfulness into your daily life, consider setting aside a few minutes each day for focused breathing or meditation. This practice can enhance your ability to be present, ultimately making you more engaging and charismatic in social situations.

Authenticity as the Core of Charisma

Above all, authenticity is the bedrock of charisma. People are instinctively drawn to those who are genuine, as it fosters trust and connection. Research from *Harvard Business School* found that authenticity significantly impacts how leaders are perceived, reinforcing the idea that being true to oneself is inherently attractive.

In my experiences, the moments when I've felt most charismatic were when I embraced my true self—flaws, quirks, and all. When you allow your authentic self to shine through, you invite others to connect with you on a deeper level. This transparency creates a sense of safety, encouraging those around you to be genuine in return.

To cultivate authenticity, reflect on your core values and beliefs. What truly matters to you? By aligning your actions with these principles, you create a consistent and genuine presence. Engage in self-discovery activities, such as journaling or deep reflection, to better understand what makes you unique.

Practical Steps to Cultivate Charisma

Practice Positive Self-Talk: Start each day with affirmations that reinforce your strengths and capabilities. Write down three things you appreciate about yourself and repeat them regularly.

Adopt Confident Body Language: Pay attention to your posture, gestures, and eye contact. Stand tall, make eye contact, and practice power poses before social interactions.

Engage in Active Listening: Focus on truly hearing what others say. Ask open-ended questions and show genuine interest in their responses.

Embrace Vulnerability: Share your experiences and challenges with others. Start with small disclosures and gradually open up more as comfort grows.

Cultivate Mindfulness: Incorporate mindfulness practices into your daily routine. Spend a few minutes each day in meditation or focused breathing to enhance your presence.

Reflect on Your Authenticity: Take time to identify your core values. Align your actions and interactions with these values to present your true self.

Foster Curiosity About Others: Approach conversations with a mindset of curiosity. Ask questions that encourage deeper discussions and connections.

Celebrate Small Wins: Recognize and celebrate your achievements, no matter how minor. This builds a sense of accomplishment and reinforces positive self-image.

Charisma is a skill that can be cultivated through awareness and practice. By shifting your mindset, embracing vulnerability, and fostering genuine connections, you can develop a magnetic presence that attracts others effortlessly. Each step taken in this journey not only enhances your ability to connect with others but also enriches your own life, creating a vibrant tapestry of relationships and experiences.

Authenticity vs. Performance

Navigating the world of charisma often brings us to a pivotal crossroads: the choice between authenticity and performance. Charisma can feel like a carefully crafted persona, a performance designed to impress. However, the essence of genuine charisma lies in authenticity—the ability to be true to oneself while engaging others. This distinction is vital for forming meaningful connections and cultivating a magnetic presence that draws people in.

Understanding Authenticity

Authenticity refers to being genuine and true to one's self, reflecting one's values, beliefs, and emotions without artifice. It's about owning who you are, with all your complexities and contradictions. Research conducted by psychologists at the *University of California* highlights that people are naturally drawn to those who display authenticity. When we present ourselves authentically, we invite others to engage more deeply, fostering trust and connection.

In my own journey, I've found that embracing authenticity has profoundly impacted my interactions. Early on, I often felt pressured to conform to certain social expectations, thinking that I had to put on a façade to be accepted. This performance-based mindset left me feeling disconnected and drained. It wasn't until I allowed myself to be vulnerable and share my true thoughts and feelings that I noticed a shift. People responded differently; they were more engaged, more interested, and ultimately more willing to connect.

Authenticity is not just about being honest; it's also about aligning our outward expressions with our inner values. This alignment fosters a sense of congruence that resonates with others. A study published in *Psychological Science* found that individuals who displayed authenticity were perceived as more likable and trustworthy. When our words and actions align with our true selves, we create a sense of reliability that is incredibly attractive.

The Allure of Performance

On the other hand, performance in social interactions can be tempting. We often feel compelled to project an image of confidence, success, and charm, particularly in high-stakes situations like job interviews or first dates. The pressure to perform can lead to a disconnect between our true selves and the personas we project.

While performance can have its place, especially in situations that require a certain level of professionalism or charisma, it can also lead to a superficial connection. When we rely solely on performance, we risk creating relationships built on façade rather than genuine connection. Research from *Harvard Business School* emphasizes that while charisma can be an effective tool for influence, it often lacks the depth of authentic engagement.

I've experienced this firsthand. In a previous role, I found myself presenting a polished, high-energy persona in meetings. On the surface, it seemed effective; people responded positively, and I achieved my goals. However, I noticed a lingering emptiness. Conversations felt transactional, and I struggled to form meaningful relationships with my colleagues. It was only when I began to integrate authenticity into my performance that I noticed a genuine shift. Sharing my struggles and uncertainties allowed others to connect with me on a deeper level, creating an environment where open dialogue flourished.

Striking the Balance

The challenge lies in striking a balance between authenticity and performance. It's possible to be genuine while still engaging in behaviors that enhance our charisma. The key is to ensure that our performances are rooted in authenticity rather than constructed solely for the sake of impression. This approach allows us to be adaptable while remaining true to ourselves.

One effective method for finding this balance is to practice situational authenticity. This means adjusting our behavior based on context while still staying aligned with our core values. For instance, in a professional setting, you may choose to present a more polished version of yourself—dressing well and using confident body language—while still sharing personal anecdotes that reflect your genuine thoughts and feelings. This blend can create an engaging dynamic that is both charismatic and authentic.

Another strategy is to develop a sense of self-awareness. Understanding our motivations, triggers, and values allows us to navigate social situations more effectively. A study from the *University of Illinois* revealed that individuals with higher self-awareness tend to build stronger relationships and exhibit greater emotional intelligence. By regularly reflecting on our experiences, we can better align our performances with our authentic selves.

The Power of Vulnerability

Vulnerability is a cornerstone of authenticity. In a society that often equates vulnerability with weakness, embracing it can be a radical act. Sharing our imperfections and insecurities creates a sense of relatability, inviting others to do the same. Research from Brené Brown emphasizes that vulnerability fosters connection; when we allow ourselves to be seen, we create an environment where others feel safe to share their truths.

In my experience, vulnerability has been a transformative element in building charismatic relationships. I've learned that when I openly discuss my challenges—be it professional setbacks or personal struggles—people respond with empathy and understanding. This openness not only enriches my interactions but also encourages others to be vulnerable in return, creating a deeper, more meaningful connection.

To practice vulnerability, start by sharing small, personal stories in social interactions. It could be a humorous mishap or a moment of uncertainty. As comfort grows, gradually share more significant experiences. This process helps to build trust and fosters a sense of intimacy that can be incredibly powerful in cultivating charisma.

The Role of Active Listening

Active listening is another vital component of authentic charisma. Engaging deeply with others not only shows that you value their perspectives but also fosters a sense of connection. Research from *The Journal of Social Psychology* indicates that effective listening enhances interpersonal relationships, making individuals feel appreciated and understood.

To practice active listening, focus entirely on the speaker. This involves eliminating distractions, maintaining eye contact, and providing verbal affirmations that indicate your engagement. Ask open-ended questions that encourage the other person to elaborate on their thoughts and feelings. This not only enriches the conversation but also creates a space where authentic connections can thrive.

In my interactions, I've made it a point to prioritize active listening. By being fully present, I've noticed that conversations flow more naturally, and I often leave interactions feeling more connected and fulfilled. This approach not only enhances my charisma but also fosters relationships that are built on mutual respect and understanding.

Embracing Imperfection

Part of embracing authenticity involves accepting our imperfections. No one is perfect, and the pressure to present an idealized version of ourselves can be stifling. Research published in *Personality and Social Psychology Bulletin* found that individuals who embrace their imperfections are often perceived as more relatable and approachable. By acknowledging our flaws, we create a space for genuine connection.

In my life, I've learned to embrace the moments of imperfection. Whether it's stumbling over my words during a presentation or admitting I don't have all the answers, these moments of vulnerability often lead to richer interactions. People appreciate honesty and are often more willing to connect when they see us as real and relatable.

To practice embracing imperfection, start by shifting your mindset around failure and mistakes. Rather than viewing them as setbacks, reframe them as opportunities for growth. Share these experiences with others, highlighting what you learned and how you've evolved. This openness fosters authenticity and encourages others to share their own experiences, deepening the connection.

The Impact of Feedback

Receiving feedback is essential for honing both authenticity and performance. Constructive feedback helps us understand how our behavior is perceived by others, allowing us to adjust accordingly while staying true to ourselves. Research from *Stanford University* emphasizes that seeking feedback enhances self-awareness and personal growth, crucial elements in developing charisma.

In my own journey, I've learned to value feedback as a tool for improvement. After presentations or social interactions, I've sought input from trusted colleagues and friends. This practice not only helps me refine my approach but also reinforces my authenticity. By understanding how my performance resonates with others, I can make adjustments while maintaining my core self.

To incorporate feedback effectively, establish a routine of asking for input after significant interactions. Be open to both positive and constructive feedback, and take time to reflect on the insights gained. This practice fosters a growth mindset and encourages ongoing development in both authenticity and charismatic presence.

Practical Steps to Cultivate Authentic Charisma

Reflect on Your Values: Take time to identify your core values and beliefs. Consider how these can guide your interactions with others, creating a foundation for authenticity.

Practice Vulnerability: Start sharing small personal anecdotes in conversations. Gradually increase the depth of your sharing as you become more comfortable.

Engage in Active Listening: Make a conscious effort to listen deeply during conversations. Maintain eye contact, nod, and ask open-ended questions to encourage dialogue.

Embrace Imperfection: Shift your perspective on failure. Share your imperfections and what you've learned from them to foster relatability and connection.

Seek Feedback: After significant interactions, ask trusted friends or colleagues for feedback on your performance and authenticity. Use this input to refine your approach.

Cultivate Self-Awareness: Regularly reflect on your interactions, motivations, and feelings. Journaling can be a useful tool for gaining insight into your authentic self.

Balance Authenticity and Performance: Identify situations where performance may be necessary, and practice situational authenticity by maintaining core values while adapting your behavior.

Develop Empathy: Practice putting yourself in others' shoes. Understanding their perspectives and emotions can enhance your ability to connect authentically.

Create a Supportive Environment: Surround yourself with people who value authenticity. Engage in communities that encourage genuine connections, allowing you to thrive as your true self.

Celebrate Progress: Acknowledge your growth in authenticity and charisma. Celebrate small wins and reflect on how far you've come in your journey toward genuine connection.

Cultivating charisma through authenticity rather than mere performance creates lasting connections that resonate deeply with others. By embracing vulnerability, practicing active listening, and balancing authenticity with situational adaptability, you can foster a charismatic presence that attracts people effortlessly. Each step taken in this journey not only enriches your interactions but also enhances your understanding of yourself.

Chapter 2: Mastering Nonverbal Communication

Body Language Basics

Body language is a silent language that speaks volumes, often conveying more than words ever could. In my journey of understanding attraction and connection, I have come to realize that mastering nonverbal communication is crucial for engaging others and fostering meaningful relationships. The nuances of body language can either enhance our presence or undermine our intentions, depending on how we use them.

• • • •

THE IMPORTANCE OF BODY Language

Research suggests that nonverbal communication accounts for a significant portion of how we interpret interactions. According to a study published in *Psychological Bulletin*, around 93% of communication effectiveness is determined by nonverbal cues. This encompasses body language, facial expressions, tone of voice, and even posture. Understanding this silent language can significantly enhance how we connect with others and create lasting impressions.

From my experience, I learned early on that the way I carried myself in social settings had a profound impact on how I was perceived. In high-stakes situations, such as job interviews or networking events, I noticed that confident body language made a difference. Standing tall, making eye contact, and using open gestures not only made me feel more self-assured but also drew others in, making them more receptive to what I had to say.

Key Elements of Body Language

Posture is one of the most foundational elements of body language. Standing or sitting up straight conveys confidence and engagement, while slouching can signal disinterest or insecurity. A study conducted by *The University of Colorado* found that individuals with open, upright postures were perceived as more confident and approachable. Practicing good posture can make a significant difference in how you are perceived by others. When I started paying attention to my posture, I noticed that people responded positively, and conversations flowed more easily.

Facial expressions are another critical component. Our faces can convey a range of emotions, often without us even realizing it. Smiling, for example, is universally understood as a sign of friendliness and approachability. Research from *The American Psychological Association* shows that a genuine smile can elicit positive feelings in others, fostering a sense of connection. When I made a conscious effort to smile more, I noticed that people were more likely to engage with me and respond positively to my presence.

Eye contact is equally vital. It conveys interest, attentiveness, and confidence. However, the amount of eye contact can vary based on cultural norms. In some cultures, too much eye contact can be perceived as aggressive, while in others, it may be seen as a sign of respect. Finding the right balance is essential. I learned this through experience; during conversations, I focused on maintaining eye contact without staring. This created an environment of trust and openness, allowing for deeper connections.

Gestures also play a crucial role in nonverbal communication. Using hand movements can help emphasize points and make conversations more engaging. However, it's essential to be mindful of how gestures are perceived. Overly animated gestures can be distracting, while minimal gestures might come across as disengaged. A study from *The University of California* highlighted that effective speakers use gestures that are natural and align with their message. I found that incorporating purposeful gestures into my communication made me appear more dynamic and confident, enhancing my overall presence.

The Power of Mirroring

Mirroring is a powerful technique in nonverbal communication that involves subtly mimicking the body language of the person you're engaging with. This can create a sense of rapport and make the other person feel more at ease. Research published in *Social Influence* found that individuals who engage in mirroring are often perceived as more likable and relatable.

In my interactions, I began to consciously practice mirroring, especially during important conversations. If someone leaned in, I would lean in slightly; if they crossed their arms, I would do the same momentarily. This technique fosters a connection that transcends words, making the other person feel understood and valued. It's a simple yet effective way to enhance rapport.

Reading Nonverbal Cues

Understanding body language is not just about projecting confidence; it also involves being attuned to the nonverbal cues of others. This skill allows us to gauge emotions and reactions, facilitating more meaningful interactions. For instance, crossed arms might indicate defensiveness, while leaning forward can signal engagement. Research in *Nonverbal Behavior* shows that being aware of these signals can significantly improve interpersonal communication.

I recall a meeting where I noticed a colleague crossing their arms and avoiding eye contact while I presented. This nonverbal cue indicated discomfort or disagreement. Instead of continuing as planned, I paused and asked for their perspective, creating an opportunity for dialogue. By being aware of their body language, I was able to foster a more inclusive environment and address any concerns that may have been simmering beneath the surface.

The Impact of Space

Proxemics, or the study of personal space, is another crucial aspect of nonverbal communication. The physical distance we maintain during interactions can convey intimacy, aggression, or social norms. Cultural differences play a significant role here. In some cultures, closer proximity is considered friendly, while in others, it may be seen as intrusive.

In my experiences, I learned to navigate these nuances by observing the comfort levels of others. In casual settings, such as gatherings with friends, I noticed that standing a bit closer fostered warmth and connection. However, in more formal environments, maintaining a respectful distance was key. This awareness of space allowed me to create an atmosphere that felt comfortable for everyone involved.

The Art of Touch

Touch is one of the most powerful forms of nonverbal communication, capable of conveying warmth, empathy, and connection. However, it's important to approach touch with sensitivity and awareness of personal boundaries. Research from *The Journal of Personality and Social Psychology* indicates that appropriate touch can enhance interpersonal connections and foster feelings of trust.

I've found that a light touch on the arm during a conversation can convey empathy and support, but context is crucial. In professional settings, it's essential to be cautious and respectful of boundaries. By being aware of the reactions of those around me, I learned when a handshake, a pat on the back, or a more personal touch might be appropriate.

Enhancing Nonverbal Skills

Mastering nonverbal communication requires practice and self-awareness. Here are practical strategies to enhance your body language skills:

Observe Yourself: Record yourself during a conversation or presentation to analyze your body language. Pay attention to posture, gestures, and facial expressions. Identifying areas for improvement can help you become more conscious of your nonverbal cues.

Practice in Low-Stakes Situations: Use casual interactions, like chatting with friends or family, to practice effective body language. Focus on maintaining good posture, eye contact, and open gestures.

Watch Others: Observe individuals you find charismatic. Pay attention to their body language and how it influences their interactions. Take note of what resonates with you and try to incorporate similar techniques.

Mirror in Conversation: Practice mirroring during conversations. Subtly adopt the other person's posture or gestures to create rapport. Be mindful not to mimic too overtly, as this can feel disingenuous.

Stay Attuned to Nonverbal Cues: Develop your ability to read the body language of others. Notice their gestures, facial expressions, and posture. Reflect on what these cues might signify in the context of your conversation.

Experiment with Proxemics: Pay attention to how close you stand to others in various contexts. Experiment with maintaining different distances and observe how it impacts the dynamics of your interactions.

Cultivate Empathy Through Touch: In appropriate settings, practice using light, respectful touch to enhance connection. Observe how it influences the response of those around you.

Create a Positive Environment: Encourage open body language in group settings by modeling it yourself. Use inclusive gestures and maintain a welcoming posture to foster an inviting atmosphere.

Practice Active Listening: Combine verbal and nonverbal cues by engaging fully with the speaker. Use nodding and encouraging facial expressions to convey your interest and support.

Be Mindful of Cultural Differences: Recognize that body language varies across cultures. Educate yourself about the norms of different cultures to avoid misunderstandings and enhance your interactions.

Developing a keen understanding of body language can transform how we communicate and connect with others. The subtleties of nonverbal cues enrich our interactions and create a magnetic presence that attracts people effortlessly. By cultivating self-awareness and practicing these skills, we can enhance our ability to engage authentically and meaningfully with those around us. Each interaction becomes an opportunity to connect on a deeper level, fostering relationships that resonate far beyond words.

The Power of Eye Contact

Eye contact holds an unparalleled power in human interactions. It can convey a multitude of emotions, from warmth and connection to confidence and authority. In my exploration of attraction and effective communication, I've learned that mastering the art of eye contact can significantly enhance how we relate to others and how they perceive us. This seemingly simple act can transform interactions, making them more engaging and memorable.

The Science Behind Eye Contact

Research shows that eye contact is crucial for effective communication. A study from *Psychological Science* indicates that people who maintain eye contact are often perceived as more trustworthy and attentive. In fact, the amount of eye contact we engage in can influence the dynamics of a conversation in profound ways. When we look someone in the eye, we signal that we are present, interested, and open to connecting.

In my early experiences, I often underestimated the impact of eye contact. During conversations, I would glance away frequently, either due to nervousness or a lack of awareness about its importance. It wasn't until I began to consciously focus on maintaining eye contact that I noticed a shift in how people responded to me. Conversations became more fluid, and I found that others seemed more engaged and willing to share.

The Benefits of Eye Contact

Establishing Connection: One of the most significant benefits of eye contact is its ability to create a sense of intimacy and connection. When we hold someone's gaze, it fosters a feeling of closeness, making the interaction more personal. Research from *The Journal of Social Psychology* emphasizes that mutual gaze increases feelings of affection and rapport between individuals.

I vividly remember a moment during a networking event where I made a conscious effort to maintain eye contact with the person I was speaking to. As I looked into their eyes, I could see their demeanor soften. They leaned in, and our conversation deepened. That moment reinforced my understanding of how eye contact can bridge the gap between strangers, creating a more inviting atmosphere.

Conveying Confidence: Eye contact is a powerful indicator of confidence. When we maintain eye contact, we project self-assuredness, which can significantly influence how others perceive us. Research from *The University of Alabama* indicates that individuals who maintain appropriate eye contact are viewed as more competent and trustworthy.

In professional settings, I found that maintaining steady eye contact during presentations or meetings made a marked difference in how my ideas were received. Colleagues appeared more engaged, and I felt more empowered in my communication. This practice of eye contact not only bolstered my confidence but also created an aura of authority that commanded respect.

Enhancing Communication: Eye contact enhances our ability to communicate effectively. It allows us to gauge the reactions of others, providing immediate feedback on how our message is being received. Research from *The Journal of Personality and Social Psychology* shows that eye contact can improve comprehension and retention of information during conversations.

When I began to pay attention to the eye contact of others while I spoke, I noticed how it guided my delivery. If someone's gaze dropped or they looked away, it often signaled that I needed to adjust my approach. By being attuned to these nonverbal cues, I became a more responsive communicator, tailoring my message to better connect with my audience.

The Right Amount of Eye Contact

Understanding the right amount of eye contact is essential. Too little can come across as disinterest, while too much may feel intimidating or aggressive. Research suggests that maintaining eye contact for about 50-70% of a conversation is ideal for creating a comfortable dynamic. This balance allows for engagement without overwhelming the other person.

In my interactions, I found that varying my eye contact based on the context helped establish a comfortable rhythm. During more serious discussions, I would maintain steady eye contact to convey sincerity. In lighter conversations, I would allow for moments of gaze diversion, creating a more relaxed atmosphere. This adaptability enhanced my ability to connect with others while respecting their comfort levels.

Cultural Differences in Eye Contact

It's crucial to recognize that the meaning of eye contact can vary significantly across cultures. In some cultures, prolonged eye contact is seen as a sign of confidence and interest, while in others, it may be viewed as disrespectful or confrontational. Understanding these cultural nuances can help prevent misunderstandings and foster more meaningful interactions.

During my travels, I encountered diverse cultural perspectives on eye contact. In Japan, for instance, people tend to avoid prolonged eye contact as a sign of respect, especially in formal settings. Adapting my approach to align with these cultural norms allowed me to connect more effectively with individuals from different backgrounds, ultimately enriching my interactions.

Techniques for Improving Eye Contact

Practice Mindfulness: Being present in conversations can significantly enhance your ability to maintain eye contact. Focus on the speaker's words, and consciously engage in making eye contact without distractions.

Start Small: If maintaining eye contact feels uncomfortable, begin by practicing in low-pressure situations. Engage with friends or family members and gradually increase the duration of eye contact as you gain confidence.

Use the Triangle Technique: To avoid staring, practice the triangle technique. Focus on one eye, then the other, and then the person's mouth. This approach helps you maintain eye contact while feeling more natural.

Be Attentive to Feedback: Pay attention to the other person's body language and reactions. If they seem uncomfortable, allow for breaks in eye contact to create a more relaxed atmosphere.

Combine Eye Contact with Smiles: Pairing eye contact with a warm smile can enhance the positive impact of your gaze. A smile can make the other person feel more at ease, fostering a sense of connection.

Practice Active Listening: Engaging in active listening requires focused eye contact. Show genuine interest by maintaining eye contact while the other person speaks, signaling your attentiveness.

Mirror the Other Person: If appropriate, subtly mirror the other person's level of eye contact. If they maintain steady eye contact, do the same. If they look away, follow suit briefly to create a sense of comfort.

Use Eye Contact in Public Speaking: When presenting to a group, practice making eye contact with different audience members. This creates a sense of inclusivity and keeps listeners engaged.

Recognize Your Comfort Zone: Understand your natural tendencies regarding eye contact. If you tend to look away frequently, consciously practice maintaining eye contact to help shift this habit.

Reflect on Your Experiences: After conversations or presentations, take time to reflect on how your eye contact impacted the interaction. Consider what worked well and what you could improve for next time.

The Role of Eye Contact in Romantic Interactions

In the realm of romance, eye contact takes on an even deeper significance. It can serve as a powerful tool for attraction, signaling interest and desire. Research published in *The Journal of Social and Personal Relationships* indicates that prolonged eye contact between romantic partners can lead to increased feelings of intimacy and connection.

I remember a moment during a date where maintaining eye contact felt effortless. As we shared stories and laughter, our gazes locked frequently, creating a palpable sense of attraction. This mutual eye contact fostered an unspoken connection that transcended words, deepening our bond in a way that felt almost magical.

In romantic settings, the nuances of eye contact become even more pronounced. A lingering gaze can communicate desire, while fleeting glances can express shyness or uncertainty. Understanding these dynamics can help navigate the complexities of romantic interactions, allowing for more profound connections.

The Impact of Eye Contact on Leadership

Eye contact plays a pivotal role in leadership as well. Leaders who use eye contact effectively are often perceived as more credible and influential. Research from *The Leadership Quarterly* shows that leaders who maintain eye contact foster trust and engagement among their teams.

In my experience as a leader, I noticed that maintaining eye contact during team meetings encouraged open dialogue. When I made a point to look at each team member while speaking, it created an environment where everyone felt valued and heard. This practice not only reinforced my role as a leader but also fostered a sense of collaboration within the team.

Overcoming Eye Contact Anxiety

For some, the prospect of maintaining eye contact can induce anxiety. It's important to acknowledge this discomfort and find ways to work through it. One effective strategy is to reframe your mindset about eye contact. Instead of viewing it as a pressure-filled expectation, consider it an opportunity to connect and engage with others.

During my journey, I encountered my own challenges with eye contact, particularly in high-stress situations. To combat this, I began to focus on the positive aspects of making eye contact. I reminded myself that it was a way to show interest and respect for the other person. Over time, this shift in perspective helped me feel more at ease and confident in my interactions.

Building Confidence Through Eye Contact

Building confidence in eye contact can be a transformative experience. The more you practice, the more natural it becomes. Start by setting small goals, such as maintaining eye contact for a few seconds longer during conversations. As you become more comfortable, gradually increase the duration, allowing yourself to revel in the connection that eye contact fosters.

In my own growth, I found that celebrating small victories—like successfully maintaining eye contact during a challenging conversation—bolstered my confidence. Acknowledging these moments reinforced the positive impact of eye contact, motivating me to continue honing this essential skill.

Mastering eye contact is an invaluable tool for enhancing communication and building connections. Whether in professional settings, social interactions, or romantic endeavors, the power of eye contact can elevate the quality of our relationships. By understanding its nuances, practicing consistently, and embracing its potential, we can foster an authentic presence that attracts others effortlessly. Eye contact becomes not just a tool for engagement but a gateway to deeper understanding and connection, enriching our lives in meaningful ways. Each interaction becomes an opportunity to connect, inspire, and thrive in the shared experience of being human.

Chapter 3: The Art of Conversation Listening to Connect

Listening is an art that often goes overlooked in the pursuit of effective communication. In my journey to understand attraction and build meaningful connections, I discovered that the quality of our listening profoundly influences the depth of our interactions. Engaging in active listening is not just about hearing words; it's about connecting on a level that fosters rapport and understanding. By honing this skill, we can transform conversations into rich exchanges that leave a lasting impression.

Understanding Active Listening

Active listening is a deliberate process that requires focus, engagement, and empathy. It involves not only hearing the words spoken but also understanding the emotions and intentions behind them. Research from the *International Journal of Listening* highlights that active listening can enhance relationships, reduce misunderstandings, and foster trust. When we listen actively, we show respect and appreciation for the speaker, paving the way for deeper connections.

Reflecting on my experiences, I remember a time when I approached a discussion with a colleague who seemed frustrated. Instead of immediately jumping in with solutions, I took a step back and focused entirely on what they were saying. This conscious effort to listen fully not only allowed me to grasp the nuances of their concerns but also made them feel valued. That interaction opened the door for a more productive dialogue and ultimately strengthened our working relationship.

Techniques for Active Listening

Be Present: The foundation of active listening is being fully present in the moment. This means putting aside distractions—whether it's your phone, a computer, or even your own thoughts. Research from *Harvard Business Review* indicates that our ability to engage deeply increases when we minimize distractions. I found that by consciously turning off notifications and giving my full attention to the speaker, I could connect with them on a deeper level.

Use Nonverbal Cues: Our body language plays a significant role in conveying that we are listening. Nodding, maintaining eye contact, and leaning slightly forward can signal engagement and interest. A study published in *The Journal of Nonverbal Behavior* underscores that nonverbal cues can reinforce the message of active listening. I made a habit of mirroring the body language of those I was speaking with, which helped create a sense of rapport and trust.

Paraphrase and Reflect: One effective technique for active listening is to paraphrase what the speaker has said. This not only shows that you are paying attention but also helps clarify any misunderstandings. For instance, if a friend expresses concern about a work project, I might respond with, "It sounds like you're feeling overwhelmed with the deadlines." This technique validates their feelings and encourages further conversation. Research in *Communication Studies* suggests that reflective listening can enhance emotional connection and understanding.

Ask Open-Ended Questions: Encouraging deeper conversation is another key aspect of active listening. Open-ended questions prompt the speaker to elaborate and share more about their thoughts and feelings. Instead of asking, "Did you have a good day?" I learned to ask, "What made your day stand out?" This simple shift invites more meaningful dialogue. Studies show that open-ended questions foster deeper connections by encouraging the speaker to explore their thoughts more fully.

Avoid Interrupting: One of the most important aspects of active listening is resisting the urge to interrupt. This can be challenging, especially when we feel a strong desire to contribute or share our perspective. Research published in *The Journal of Applied Communication Research* highlights that interruptions can lead to feelings of frustration and disengagement in conversations. I trained myself to wait until the speaker finished before responding, which allowed them to express themselves fully. This patience often resulted in more thoughtful and productive exchanges.

Empathize with the Speaker: Empathy is a cornerstone of effective listening. It involves putting yourself in the speaker's shoes and understanding their emotions and perspectives. Studies in *The Journal of Personality and Social Psychology* indicate that empathetic listening fosters a stronger connection and enhances relationship quality. When a friend shares a difficult experience, I focus on acknowledging their feelings by saying things like, "I can imagine how challenging that must be for you." This practice not only validates their emotions but also deepens our connection.

Use Affirmative Responses: Verbal affirmations, such as "I see" or "That makes sense," can encourage the speaker to continue sharing. These simple phrases signal that you are engaged and interested in their narrative. Research in *Interpersonal Communication* suggests that affirmative responses can help maintain the flow of conversation and make the speaker feel valued. I incorporated these affirmations into my interactions, noticing how they positively influenced the dynamics of the conversation.

Be Mindful of Your Own Responses: During conversations, it's essential to be aware of your own emotions and reactions. If you find yourself feeling defensive or overwhelmed, take a moment to breathe and refocus. Research in *The Journal of Experimental Social Psychology* indicates that emotional self-awareness can improve communication and foster healthier interactions. I practiced grounding techniques, such as deep breathing, to maintain a calm presence, allowing me to listen without being influenced by my own emotional state.

Practice Active Listening in Everyday Conversations: Integrating active listening into daily interactions can help reinforce this skill. Whether chatting with a friend, a colleague, or even a cashier, making a conscious effort to listen actively can transform even the most mundane exchanges. I started viewing every conversation as an opportunity to practice my listening skills. The more I applied these techniques, the more natural they became, enhancing my overall ability to connect with others.

Follow Up After Conversations: Following up after a conversation can show the speaker that you value what they shared. A simple message or note expressing appreciation for their insights can reinforce your connection. Research from *The Journal of Business Communication* highlights that follow-up communication enhances relationship-building and trust. I began to send quick texts after significant conversations, expressing gratitude for their openness, which deepened our rapport over time.

Listening to Build Rapport

Building rapport is about creating a sense of connection and mutual understanding. Active listening is a powerful tool in this process, allowing us to establish trust and foster meaningful relationships. When we make a conscious effort to listen, we signal to others that their thoughts and feelings matter, paving the way for deeper interactions.

In my own life, I recall a moment when I was attending a social event where I felt a bit out of place. I approached a small group engaged in conversation and decided to practice active listening. By asking open-ended questions and genuinely focusing on their responses, I was able to connect with them more easily. They welcomed my engagement, and before I knew it, I had built rapport and felt included in their conversation. This experience underscored the importance of listening as a means to forge connections in unfamiliar settings.

Listening as a Leadership Skill

In leadership, the ability to listen effectively is paramount. Good leaders recognize that active listening fosters collaboration and empowers team members. Research from *The Center for Creative Leadership* emphasizes that leaders who listen actively are perceived as more effective and approachable.

In my experience, I found that fostering a culture of active listening within my team led to increased morale and productivity. During team meetings, I made it a point to ask for input and genuinely listen to the perspectives of my colleagues. This practice not only encouraged open dialogue but also cultivated an environment where everyone felt valued and heard.

Listening in Romantic Relationships

Active listening also plays a crucial role in romantic relationships. Partners who practice active listening are better equipped to navigate conflicts and strengthen their emotional connection. Research published in *The Journal of Marriage and Family* indicates that couples who engage in active listening report higher relationship satisfaction.

I've noticed that during disagreements with my partner, taking the time to actively listen to their perspective can defuse tension. Instead of immediately jumping to conclusions or defending my point of view, I focus on understanding their feelings and concerns. This approach often leads to more constructive discussions and reinforces our bond.

Overcoming Barriers to Active Listening

Despite its importance, several barriers can hinder effective listening. External distractions, personal biases, and emotional reactions can all disrupt our ability to engage fully. Recognizing these barriers is the first step in overcoming them.

I found that creating an optimal listening environment can significantly enhance my ability to listen actively. This could mean choosing a quiet space for important conversations or ensuring that I'm emotionally grounded before engaging with someone. By being aware of these barriers, I've been able to cultivate a more receptive mindset, allowing for deeper connections.

Cultivating a Listening Mindset

Developing a listening mindset involves embracing curiosity and openness in conversations. When we approach interactions with a genuine desire to understand, we naturally become better listeners. Research in *Psychology Today* suggests that cultivating a mindset of curiosity can enhance our communication skills and strengthen our relationships.

I started to view each conversation as an opportunity to learn something new. This shift in perspective helped me engage more deeply with others, fostering a genuine connection. By focusing on understanding rather than responding, I discovered the richness of conversations and the insights they could offer.

Listening and Personal Growth

Active listening not only enhances our relationships but also contributes to personal growth. Engaging with diverse perspectives broadens our understanding of the world and deepens our empathy. Research published in *The Journal of Applied Psychology* highlights that effective listening can lead to greater emotional intelligence and interpersonal skills.

Reflecting on my experiences, I realized that each interaction provides an opportunity for growth. By actively listening to others, I've been able to gain insights into their lives and experiences, which has enriched my own understanding of human connection. This commitment to listening has become a cornerstone of my personal development journey.

The Ripple Effect of Active Listening

The impact of active listening extends beyond individual interactions. When we practice active listening, we create a ripple effect that influences the dynamics of our relationships and communities. Research in *Social Psychology* suggests that positive listening behaviors can encourage others to reciprocate, fostering a culture of connection and understanding.

I've seen this ripple effect firsthand. When I prioritize active listening, those around me tend to respond in kind. This creates an environment where open dialogue and mutual respect thrive, enhancing the quality of our interactions.

Listening as a Lifelong Skill

Ultimately, active listening is a skill that requires continuous practice and refinement. The more we engage in active listening, the more natural it becomes, allowing us to forge deeper connections with others. Embracing this skill as a lifelong endeavor can lead to more fulfilling relationships and a greater understanding of the world around us.

In my own journey, I've found that committing to active listening has profoundly transformed my interactions. Each conversation becomes an opportunity to connect, learn, and grow, enriching both my life and the lives of those I engage with. As we cultivate the art of listening, we unlock the potential for authentic connections that resonate far beyond the moment.

The Balance of Give and Take

Navigating the flow of conversation is an intricate dance that requires an understanding of dynamics, awareness of cues, and a genuine desire to connect. Throughout my experiences, I've learned that successful conversations hinge on a delicate balance of give and take. It's not just about talking; it's about sharing the space of dialogue in a way that fosters mutual engagement and understanding.

The Dynamics of Conversation

Conversations often follow a natural ebb and flow, where one person speaks, and the other listens, responds, and shares. Research from *The Journal of Language and Social Psychology* emphasizes that effective communication is largely about timing and responsiveness. Conversations become engaging when both parties actively participate, contributing their thoughts while remaining attuned to the other's contributions.

In my early attempts at engaging conversations, I often found myself dominating discussions. Eager to share my experiences and opinions, I neglected the importance of allowing others to contribute. It wasn't until I recognized the value of listening and inviting others into the dialogue that I began to see the transformative power of balanced conversations. The simple act of stepping back to create space for others changed the quality of my interactions dramatically.

Recognizing Cues

One of the keys to achieving balance in conversation is being attuned to verbal and nonverbal cues. Body language, tone of voice, and facial expressions can all signal how engaged the other person is. Research from *Psychological Science* indicates that nonverbal cues play a crucial role in communication, often conveying more than words alone.

For instance, during a conversation with a colleague who appeared restless and distracted, I noticed their body language signaling disengagement. Rather than continuing to speak, I paused and asked if they were feeling overwhelmed. This small adjustment not only demonstrated my awareness but also invited them to share their thoughts. By recognizing these cues, I learned to navigate the conversation flow more effectively.

The Importance of Asking Questions

Questions are a powerful tool for balancing give and take. Open-ended questions invite deeper responses and create opportunities for the other person to share their thoughts and feelings. Research from *The Journal of Experimental Social Psychology* suggests that open questions foster greater engagement and rapport.

When I began to incorporate more open-ended questions into my conversations, I noticed a significant shift in how people responded. Instead of merely answering yes or no, they started to elaborate on their experiences. For example, rather than asking, "Did you enjoy the event?" I shifted to, "What stood out to you most about the event?" This simple change encouraged a richer exchange and allowed the conversation to flow naturally.

The Art of Paraphrasing

Paraphrasing is another effective technique for maintaining the balance of conversation. By summarizing what the other person has said, you not only demonstrate that you are listening but also provide them an opportunity to clarify their thoughts. Research from *The International Journal of Listening* highlights that paraphrasing can enhance understanding and strengthen connections.

In practice, I found that paraphrasing allowed me to reinforce the speaker's message. For instance, during a discussion about personal goals, I might say, "So you're saying that you want to focus on your career development while also making time for family, right?" This approach encourages the speaker to confirm or elaborate further, enriching the conversation and ensuring that both parties are on the same page.

Timing and Rhythm

Every conversation has its rhythm, influenced by the pacing and timing of responses. Interruptions can disrupt this flow, leading to frustration or disengagement. Research published in *Communication Research* indicates that timing plays a critical role in conversational satisfaction.

I learned to pay attention to the natural pauses in conversation. When the other person takes a breath or shows a moment of contemplation, it's often an invitation for me to step in or ask a question. Conversely, if I noticed they were on a roll, I'd practice patience and allow them to finish their thoughts. This awareness of timing creates a seamless flow, where both parties feel valued and understood.

The Give and Take of Sharing

Sharing personal anecdotes and experiences can enhance the conversational flow, but it's essential to find the right balance. Conversations can quickly tilt if one person overshares or monopolizes the dialogue. Research from *Social Psychology* suggests that effective conversations are characterized by an equitable exchange of personal stories and insights.

When I engage in conversations, I strive to share relevant experiences that relate to the topic at hand. For example, if a friend is discussing a recent travel experience, I might share a similar story from my own travels. However, I've learned to be mindful of not overshadowing their narrative. Acknowledging their experience first before introducing my own fosters a sense of connection and encourages them to keep sharing.

The Role of Empathy

Empathy is a powerful force in conversations, allowing us to connect on a deeper level. When we empathize with the other person's feelings or experiences, we create a safe space for open dialogue. Research published in *The Journal of Personality and Social Psychology* underscores that empathetic listening can enhance relational satisfaction and foster trust.

I've found that expressing empathy often opens the door to richer discussions. When a friend shares a challenge they're facing, instead of immediately offering solutions, I respond with understanding. A simple statement like, "That sounds really tough; I can see why you'd feel that way," not only validates their feelings but also invites them to elaborate further. This empathetic approach deepens the connection and encourages a balanced exchange.

Navigating Awkward Pauses

Awkward pauses can sometimes disrupt the flow of conversation, leading to discomfort. However, rather than seeing these moments as negative, I've learned to embrace them as opportunities for reflection. Research in *The Journal of Communication* suggests that pauses can enhance conversation quality by allowing both parties to process what has been said.

When I encounter a pause, I focus on maintaining a relaxed demeanor. Instead of rushing to fill the silence, I use that time to reflect on the conversation. I might ask a follow-up question or share a related thought, which often leads to more profound insights. Embracing these pauses can create a comfortable space for both parties to gather their thoughts and enhance the overall dialogue.

Balancing Assertiveness and Receptiveness

In conversations, it's essential to strike a balance between assertiveness and receptiveness. While it's important to express your thoughts and opinions, it's equally vital to remain open to the perspectives of others. Research from *The Journal of Social Issues* emphasizes that effective communicators are those who can assert their views while also being receptive to feedback.

I've found that practicing assertive communication has enriched my conversations. Instead of shying away from expressing my opinions, I share my thoughts while remaining open to differing viewpoints. For example, during a discussion about current events, I might express my perspective and invite others to share theirs. This balance creates a space for constructive dialogue, where all voices are heard and respected.

Recognizing the Influence of Context

The context of a conversation can significantly influence the flow and dynamics. Factors such as the setting, the relationship between participants, and the subject matter can all affect how we navigate dialogue. Research from *Communication Theory* highlights that context plays a pivotal role in shaping conversation outcomes.

I learned to adapt my conversational style based on the context. In professional settings, I might adopt a more structured approach, while in casual gatherings, I feel free to explore topics more fluidly. Recognizing these contextual cues allows me to tailor my engagement, enhancing the overall conversation experience for both parties.

Practicing Reflection

After conversations, reflecting on the exchange can provide valuable insights into your conversational style and effectiveness. Taking time to consider what worked well and what could be improved can enhance future interactions. Research from *The Journal of Applied Psychology* suggests that reflective practice can lead to better interpersonal skills over time.

I developed a habit of reflecting on significant conversations, whether they were with friends, colleagues, or acquaintances. I would ask myself questions like, "Did I listen as much as I spoke?" or "How did the other person respond to my questions?" This self-reflection helped me identify areas for growth and reinforced the importance of maintaining balance in future conversations.

The Power of Vulnerability

Vulnerability can play a crucial role in establishing a balanced conversation. When we share our experiences and emotions authentically, we invite others to do the same. Research published in

The Journal of Humanistic Psychology emphasizes that vulnerability fosters deeper connections and trust in relationships.

In my interactions, I've found that being open about my own challenges or uncertainties encourages others to reciprocate. For example, during a discussion about career aspirations, I might share my own struggles and doubts. This openness creates an environment where both parties feel comfortable sharing their vulnerabilities, resulting in a more authentic exchange.

Encouraging Mutual Engagement

Encouraging mutual engagement is vital for maintaining a balanced conversation. This involves creating opportunities for the other person to share their thoughts while also contributing your own. Research from *The Journal of Communication* highlights that mutual engagement enhances relational satisfaction and fosters a sense of partnership.

I learned to invite others into the dialogue by explicitly asking for their opinions or experiences. For instance, during a brainstorming session with colleagues, I would prompt, "What are your thoughts on this idea?" This approach not only encourages participation but also reinforces the idea that everyone's input is valuable. By actively seeking engagement, I created a more collaborative atmosphere that enhanced the overall conversation.

Balancing Humor and Seriousness

The tone of a conversation can significantly impact its flow and engagement. Humor can lighten the mood and create a sense of camaraderie, while serious topics may require a more thoughtful approach. Research published in *Humor: International Journal of Humor Research* indicates that appropriate humor can enhance interpersonal relationships and foster a positive communication climate.

I discovered that incorporating humor into conversations can be a powerful tool for balance. During lighter discussions, I often share anecdotes or lighthearted observations that invite laughter. Conversely, in more serious conversations, I focus on maintaining a respectful and empathetic tone. Finding the right balance between humor and seriousness creates a dynamic that keeps conversations engaging and enjoyable.

Cultivating Mindfulness in Conversation

Mindfulness plays a crucial role in achieving balance during conversations. Being present and attentive allows us to engage fully with the other person and respond authentically. Research from *Mindfulness* emphasizes that mindfulness practices can enhance communication skills and interpersonal effectiveness.

I began incorporating mindfulness techniques into my conversations, such as focusing on my breath before engaging in dialogue. This practice helped me ground myself and remain present during exchanges. By cultivating mindfulness, I noticed a marked improvement in my ability to listen actively and respond thoughtfully, enriching the overall quality of my conversations.

Developing Confidence in Conversation

Confidence is essential for navigating the flow of conversation effectively. When we approach conversations with self-assurance, we create an environment that encourages open dialogue. Research from *The Journal of Personality and Social Psychology* underscores that confidence in communication enhances relational dynamics and satisfaction.

I found that building my confidence involved a combination of preparation and practice. Before engaging in significant conversations, I would reflect on my thoughts and experiences related to the topic. This preparation helped me feel more assured and articulate, allowing for a more fluid exchange. Additionally, the more I practiced these skills in various contexts, the more confident I became in navigating the conversational flow.

The Continuous Journey of Conversation

Ultimately, the art of conversation is a lifelong journey that requires ongoing practice, reflection, and adaptation. Each interaction presents an opportunity to refine our skills and deepen our connections with others. By embracing the balance of give and take, we open ourselves to richer dialogues and more meaningful relationships.

In my experiences, I've discovered that every conversation offers valuable lessons. By approaching conversations with curiosity and a willingness to learn, I've been able to cultivate more fulfilling interactions. As we navigate the complexities of communication, the balance of give and take remains a guiding principle that enhances our ability to connect effortlessly with others.

Chapter 4: Building Emotional Intelligence Understanding Emotions

Emotional intelligence (EI) is a powerful tool that enhances our ability to connect with others, navigate social complexities, and respond effectively to various situations. Recognizing and responding to emotions—both our own and those of others—can profoundly impact our relationships and overall interpersonal dynamics. Throughout my experiences, I've seen how cultivating emotional intelligence not only enriches our interactions but also transforms the way we engage with the world around us.

The Nature of Emotions

Emotions are multifaceted experiences that encompass physiological responses, psychological states, and behavioral reactions. Understanding emotions begins with recognizing their complexity. Research from the *Journal of Personality and Social Psychology* indicates that emotions can vary greatly in intensity and duration, influenced by a multitude of factors, including context, personal history, and cultural background.

In my journey to develop emotional intelligence, I often found myself reflecting on my own emotional responses. For instance, during a particularly stressful day at work, I noticed my frustration building. Rather than letting this emotion dictate my interactions, I took a moment to acknowledge what I was feeling. This self-awareness allowed me to approach my colleagues with a clearer mindset rather than projecting my stress onto them.

The Importance of Self-Awareness

Self-awareness is the cornerstone of emotional intelligence. By understanding our own emotions, we can better manage our reactions and interactions. Research published in *Emotional Intelligence* emphasizes that individuals with high self-awareness are more effective communicators and relationship builders.

I began to practice self-reflection regularly, keeping a journal to track my emotions and responses throughout the day. This practice helped me identify patterns in my emotional responses. For example, I realized that certain situations triggered feelings of inadequacy, which affected my interactions. By acknowledging these triggers, I could prepare myself better for future encounters, allowing me to respond more thoughtfully.

Recognizing Emotions in Others

The ability to recognize emotions in others is a critical aspect of emotional intelligence. This involves being attuned to verbal and nonverbal cues, such as tone of voice, facial expressions, and body language. Research from *Psychological Science* underscores that people often communicate their emotions through subtle cues, which can be easily overlooked.

In conversations, I started to pay closer attention to how people expressed their feelings. During one meeting, a colleague presented an idea but seemed unusually quiet and hesitant. Instead of pushing ahead with the agenda, I paused and asked, "How do you feel about this idea?" This simple question opened the door for them to express their uncertainty, leading to a more collaborative discussion. Recognizing their hesitation not only built trust but also encouraged a more open exchange of ideas.

• • • •

EMPATHY AS A TOOL

Empathy is a key component of emotional intelligence that allows us to connect deeply with others. It involves understanding and sharing the feelings of another person, which fosters trust and rapport. Research from *The Journal of Experimental Social Psychology* highlights that empathetic individuals are often better at navigating social interactions and resolving conflicts.

I remember a time when a close friend experienced a significant loss. Instead of offering platitudes, I focused on being present and empathetic. I asked open-ended questions, such as, "What has been the hardest part for you?" This approach allowed my friend to share their feelings without feeling pressured to respond in a certain way. By practicing empathy, I created a safe space for them to express their emotions, which deepened our friendship.

Active Listening

Active listening is a crucial skill for understanding and responding to others' emotions effectively. It requires not only hearing the words spoken but also engaging with the underlying feelings and meanings. Research published in *The International Journal of Listening* emphasizes that active listening fosters a deeper connection and improves communication.

I began incorporating active listening techniques into my conversations. This included maintaining eye contact, nodding, and paraphrasing what the speaker said to confirm my understanding. For instance, during a discussion with a coworker who felt overwhelmed by deadlines, I might say, "It sounds like you're feeling really stressed about the upcoming project." This acknowledgment of their feelings not only validated their experience but also encouraged them to share more. The practice of active listening became a powerful tool in my emotional intelligence toolkit.

Nonverbal Communication

Understanding nonverbal communication is essential for recognizing emotions. Body language, facial expressions, and gestures often convey feelings more accurately than words. Research in *The Journal of Nonverbal Behavior* indicates that nonverbal cues can enhance our understanding of emotional states and intentions.

I started to be more observant of nonverbal signals in my interactions. For example, I noticed that when a colleague crossed their arms and avoided eye contact during a discussion, they might be feeling defensive or uncomfortable. Instead of pressing forward, I would gently ask if they wanted to share their perspective. Being attuned to these nonverbal cues helped me create a more supportive environment, allowing others to express their emotions freely.

Responding Appropriately

Once we recognize emotions in others, the next step is responding appropriately. This involves being mindful of how our words and actions can influence the emotional climate of a conversation. Research from *The Journal of Social Psychology* emphasizes that thoughtful responses can foster connection and understanding.

During a recent conversation with a friend who was frustrated with a work situation, I practiced mindful responding. Instead of offering immediate solutions, I acknowledged their feelings by saying, "It sounds like you're really frustrated with how things are going." This simple validation made my friend feel heard and appreciated, allowing them to continue expressing their thoughts. By responding with empathy and understanding, I contributed to a more constructive dialogue.

Practicing Emotional Regulation

Emotional regulation is the ability to manage and respond to emotional experiences effectively. This skill is crucial for maintaining healthy relationships and navigating challenging situations. Research published in *Cognitive Therapy and Research* suggests that individuals with strong emotional regulation skills are better equipped to handle stress and interpersonal conflicts.

I began to implement emotional regulation strategies in my life. When I felt overwhelmed or triggered, I practiced techniques such as deep breathing and mindfulness to center myself. For instance, during a heated discussion, I would take a moment to breathe deeply and refocus before responding. This practice allowed me to approach conversations with a clearer mind and a more balanced emotional state, reducing the likelihood of reactive responses.

The Power of Validation

Validation is a powerful tool in building emotional connections. It involves acknowledging and affirming another person's feelings, helping them feel understood and supported. Research from *The Journal of Family Psychology* highlights that validation can significantly enhance emotional intimacy in relationships.

I learned to practice validation regularly. When a friend expressed anxiety about a life decision, I would respond with, "It's completely understandable to feel that way given the circumstances." This validation not only reassured them but also encouraged them to share more about their concerns. By incorporating validation into my interactions, I fostered deeper emotional connections and created a more supportive environment.

Building Trust Through Emotional Intelligence

Emotional intelligence plays a vital role in building trust in relationships. When we demonstrate an understanding of others' emotions and respond with empathy, we create a foundation of trust and respect. Research from *The Journal of Business and Psychology* underscores that high emotional intelligence contributes to stronger relationships in both personal and professional contexts.

In my experiences, I found that being emotionally attuned to others built trust over time. Colleagues began to confide in me about their challenges, knowing that I would listen without judgment. This trust led to more open communication and collaboration, resulting in a more cohesive team dynamic. By prioritizing emotional intelligence, I created an environment where everyone felt valued and heard.

Recognizing Cultural Differences

Cultural differences can significantly influence emotional expression and interpretation. Different cultures have varying norms regarding emotional expression, which can lead to misunderstandings if not recognized. Research from *Cultural Psychology* highlights the importance of cultural awareness in emotional intelligence.

I became more aware of these cultural nuances in my interactions. For example, while working with a diverse team, I noticed that some members expressed emotions more openly than others. By adapting my approach and being sensitive to these differences, I could foster a more inclusive environment. Asking questions and being curious about others' emotional expressions helped me navigate these cultural differences effectively.

The Role of Feedback

Feedback is an essential component of developing emotional intelligence. It allows us to gain insights into how our emotional responses affect others and how we can improve our interactions. Research from *The Journal of Applied Psychology* indicates that constructive feedback enhances emotional awareness and interpersonal effectiveness.

I made it a habit to seek feedback from trusted friends and colleagues about my emotional responses. After significant conversations, I would ask questions like, "How did my response make you feel?" This practice helped me understand how my emotions influenced others' experiences, allowing me to adjust my approach for future interactions. Embracing feedback became a valuable part of my journey in building emotional intelligence.

Developing Compassionate Communication

Compassionate communication emphasizes empathy, understanding, and respect in our interactions. It involves expressing ourselves authentically while being sensitive to the emotions of others. Research from *The Journal of Compassionate Healthcare* highlights that compassionate communication can enhance emotional connections and overall well-being.

I began to incorporate compassionate communication techniques into my conversations. When discussing sensitive topics, I focused on using "I" statements to express my feelings while being mindful of the other person's emotions. For example, instead of saying, "You never listen to me," I would say, "I feel unheard when I don't get a chance to share my thoughts." This approach minimized defensiveness and encouraged open dialogue, leading to more productive conversations.

Continuous Learning and Growth

Building emotional intelligence is an ongoing process that requires continuous learning and self-reflection. As we encounter new experiences and relationships, we have the opportunity to refine our emotional skills. Research published in *Personality and Social Psychology Bulletin* emphasizes that individuals who actively seek to improve their emotional intelligence experience greater satisfaction in their relationships.

I committed to lifelong learning in this area, exploring books, workshops, and online resources focused on emotional intelligence. Engaging with diverse perspectives and experiences enriched my understanding of emotions and their impact on relationships. This commitment to growth allowed me to adapt my emotional intelligence skills to various contexts, enhancing my ability to connect with others.

The Impact of Emotional Intelligence on Relationships

Ultimately, developing emotional intelligence can profoundly impact our relationships, enabling us to connect with others on a deeper level. By recognizing and responding to emotions—both our own and those of others—we create an environment of understanding, trust, and compassion.

Throughout my journey, I've seen the transformative power of emotional intelligence in my interactions. By prioritizing self-awareness, empathy, and effective communication, I've cultivated relationships that are richer, more fulfilling, and built on a foundation of emotional understanding. As we continue to explore the depths of our emotional experiences, we unlock the potential for authentic connections that resonate far beyond the moment.

Empathy in Action

Empathy is often hailed as the cornerstone of emotional intelligence, a powerful tool that enables us to forge deeper connections with others. It goes beyond simply understanding someone else's feelings; empathy requires us to engage with those emotions in a way that fosters trust, compassion, and mutual respect. Through my personal experiences and insights from recent research, I have come to appreciate how empathy can transform our relationships and enhance our ability to connect with others on a profound level.

Understanding Empathy

Empathy involves recognizing, understanding, and responding to the emotions of others. It can be broken down into two primary components: cognitive empathy, which is the ability to understand another's perspective, and emotional empathy, which is the capacity to share and resonate with someone's feelings. Research published in the journal *Frontiers in Psychology* highlights that both forms of empathy are crucial for effective interpersonal communication and relationship-building.

In my journey to cultivate empathy, I learned to pay attention to both aspects. Cognitive empathy allowed me to grasp the complexities of what someone was experiencing, while emotional empathy helped me connect on a more visceral level. For example, when a friend confided in me about their struggles with anxiety, I made a conscious effort to not only understand their feelings but to also share in that emotional space, creating a sense of solidarity that deepened our connection.

The Role of Active Listening

Active listening is an essential skill that enhances our ability to empathize with others. This involves fully concentrating, understanding, responding, and then remembering what is being said. Research from *The International Journal of Listening* emphasizes that active listening promotes a sense of safety and validation in conversations, allowing individuals to express themselves more freely.

I found that when I engaged in active listening, I was better able to tune into the emotions being conveyed. During conversations, I would maintain eye contact, nod affirmatively, and reflect back what I heard. For instance, when a colleague expressed frustration about a project, I responded with, "It sounds like you're feeling overwhelmed and unsupported." This validation not only showed that I was listening but also encouraged them to share more, creating an environment where emotional expression was welcomed.

Practicing Nonverbal Empathy

Nonverbal communication plays a significant role in conveying empathy. Our body language, facial expressions, and tone of voice can all signal our understanding and support. Research published in *The Journal of Nonverbal Behavior* highlights that nonverbal cues can significantly enhance the emotional quality of our interactions.

I began to be more mindful of my nonverbal communication when interacting with others. For example, leaning slightly forward while someone was speaking signaled my interest and engagement. Additionally, mirroring their expressions—such as smiling when they shared something positive or adopting a concerned look during challenging moments—created a powerful connection. This nonverbal empathy reinforced the message that I was not just hearing their words but genuinely resonating with their feelings.

• • • •

CULTIVATING COMPASSION

Compassion is an extension of empathy, characterized by a desire to alleviate another person's suffering. It involves not just understanding someone's feelings but also being motivated to help them in some way. Research from *The Journal of Compassionate*

Healthcare underscores the importance of compassion in building strong relationships.

I discovered that practicing compassion often meant being proactive in my interactions. For instance, when a friend shared their struggles, rather than simply listening, I would ask how I could help. This could be as simple as offering to help with a task or being available for a follow-up conversation. By taking action, I not only demonstrated my empathy but also fostered a deeper connection through shared experiences and support.

The Power of Vulnerability

Emotional vulnerability can strengthen connections and enhance empathy. When we allow ourselves to be vulnerable, we create an environment where others feel safe to share their own feelings. Research published in *The Journal of Humanistic Psychology* indicates that vulnerability fosters intimacy and trust in relationships.

I learned to embrace vulnerability in my interactions. Sharing my own challenges and fears often opened the door for others to do the same. For instance, during a discussion about career setbacks, I might share my own experiences of failure. This act of vulnerability not only deepened our conversation but also established a sense of mutual understanding and support.

Responding with Empathy

Once we recognize the emotions of others, responding with empathy is crucial. This means acknowledging their feelings and expressing understanding in a way that resonates. Research from *The Journal of Personality and Social Psychology* emphasizes that empathetic responses can significantly enhance interpersonal relationships.

When a friend expressed sadness over a personal loss, I didn't rush to offer solutions or try to cheer them up. Instead, I said, "I can't imagine how painful this must be for you right now." This simple acknowledgment of their feelings communicated my empathy and invited them to share more about their experience. By allowing space for their emotions, I fostered a deeper connection that encouraged further dialogue.

The Impact of Empathy on Conflict Resolution

Empathy can play a crucial role in conflict resolution by fostering understanding and reducing defensiveness. When we approach disagreements with empathy, we create an opportunity for constructive dialogue. Research published in *Conflict Resolution Quarterly* indicates that empathetic communication can significantly enhance conflict resolution outcomes.

I have experienced this firsthand in both personal and professional conflicts. When disagreements arose, I made a conscious effort to listen to the other person's perspective without interruption. Acknowledging their feelings, even if I disagreed, often diffused tension. For example, during a team meeting where opinions clashed, I would say, "I understand that this issue is very important to you. Can you help me understand your viewpoint better?" This empathetic approach created an atmosphere of collaboration, paving the way for effective problem-solving.

Building Emotional Resilience Through Empathy

Empathy not only enhances our connections with others but also fosters our emotional resilience. When we practice empathy, we build stronger support networks, which can help us navigate life's challenges. Research from *The Journal of Social Issues* highlights that individuals with strong social connections are better equipped to handle stress and adversity.

I found that by being empathetic toward others, I also cultivated a sense of community and support for myself. When I invested time in understanding others' struggles, I often discovered that they were willing to reciprocate. During times of personal difficulty, having these strong connections made it easier for me to seek help and support. This reciprocal nature of empathy created a network of emotional resilience that strengthened my overall well-being.

The Role of Empathy in Leadership

In professional settings, empathy is increasingly recognized as a vital leadership quality. Leaders who demonstrate empathy can foster a positive work environment, enhance team dynamics, and promote employee satisfaction. Research published in *The Journal of Leadership Studies* emphasizes that empathetic leaders are more effective in motivating and engaging their teams.

In my own leadership experiences, I found that practicing empathy significantly improved my relationships with team members. During performance reviews, I made it a point to listen to their concerns and aspirations, acknowledging their feelings about their roles. This approach not only built trust but also empowered them to express their needs and challenges openly. By fostering an empathetic work culture, I created an environment where individuals felt valued and motivated to contribute.

Teaching Empathy to Others

Empathy can be cultivated and taught, making it a valuable skill for enhancing interpersonal relationships. Research from *The Journal of Educational Psychology* indicates that programs focused on developing empathy in students lead to improved social interactions and reduced aggression.

I began to explore ways to share empathy-building practices with those around me. In group settings, I encouraged exercises that involved sharing personal stories or perspectives on various topics. This practice not only fostered deeper understanding but also created a culture of empathy within the group. By modeling empathetic behavior, I inspired others to engage more deeply in their interactions, ultimately enriching our collective experience.

The Challenges of Empathy

While empathy is a powerful tool, it can also be challenging to practice consistently. Emotional fatigue, for instance, can arise when we absorb the feelings of others without adequate self-care. Research published in *Emotion* emphasizes the importance of balancing empathy with self-care to prevent burnout.

I experienced this challenge during a particularly emotionally charged period when multiple friends faced significant hardships. I found myself feeling overwhelmed by their struggles. Recognizing this, I began to set boundaries around my emotional energy. I learned to practice self-care, allowing myself time to recharge. This balance enabled me to continue being empathetic without becoming emotionally drained, ensuring that I could support others without sacrificing my well-being.

Expanding Empathy Beyond Close Relationships

Empathy is not limited to close relationships; it can also extend to acquaintances and even strangers. Expanding our empathetic reach can create a more compassionate world. Research from *The Journal of Social Issues* indicates that practicing empathy toward diverse individuals can lead to greater social cohesion and understanding.

I made a conscious effort to practice empathy in everyday encounters, such as while interacting with service workers or fellow commuters. Acknowledging the stress or challenges they might be facing—whether through a warm smile or a friendly comment—often opened the door to brief yet meaningful connections. By consciously choosing to extend empathy beyond my immediate circle, I contributed to a more compassionate environment and discovered the beauty in these small, shared moments.

Continuous Growth in Empathy

Building empathy is an ongoing journey that requires self-reflection, practice, and commitment. The more we actively engage in empathetic behavior, the more naturally it becomes part of our interactions. Research from *The Journal of Positive Psychology* highlights that individuals who cultivate empathy report higher levels of life satisfaction and well-being.

I recognized that empathy is a skill that requires continuous nurturing. I committed to reading about empathy, attending workshops, and engaging in discussions about emotional intelligence. This commitment to growth allowed me to deepen my understanding of empathy and its role in building connections. Each experience reinforced the importance of empathy in my life, enriching my relationships and enhancing my ability to connect with others authentically.

The Ripple Effect of Empathy

The impact of empathy extends beyond individual interactions; it has the potential to create a ripple effect in our communities. When we practice empathy, we inspire others to do the same, fostering a culture of understanding and compassion. Research from *The Journal of Community Psychology* emphasizes that empathetic behaviors can lead to increased prosocial actions within communities.

I witnessed this firsthand in my community when a group of individuals came together to support a local charity. The shared commitment to understanding the struggles of others created an atmosphere of kindness and generosity. Each act of empathy—whether through volunteering time, donating resources, or simply sharing encouraging words—contributed to a greater sense of belonging and connection. This ripple effect demonstrated how empathy can foster a collective spirit of compassion, enriching our shared experiences.

As we continue to explore and develop our empathy, we unlock the potential for deeper connections that resonate far beyond individual interactions. Through active listening, compassionate responses, and a commitment to understanding the emotions of others, we can build relationships that are richer, more meaningful, and grounded in mutual respect. In a world that often feels disconnected, empathy serves as a powerful antidote, allowing us to forge authentic connections and create a more compassionate society.

Chapter 5: Enhancing Your Presence
The Role of Humor

Laughter has an extraordinary power to bridge gaps between people, transforming a mundane encounter into a memorable experience. When used effectively, humor can create an inviting atmosphere that fosters connection, ease, and trust. Through my personal experiences and insights gathered from recent research, I have come to appreciate humor as an essential tool for enhancing one's presence and attracting others effortlessly.

The Science of Laughter

Humor is more than just a source of amusement; it plays a crucial role in our psychological and physiological well-being. Research published in the journal *Psychological Science* reveals that laughter can reduce stress, enhance mood, and even strengthen social bonds. When we laugh, our bodies release endorphins, creating a sense of joy and relaxation. This biological response not only makes us feel good but also makes us more approachable and relatable to others.

I first noticed the effects of laughter during a networking event where I felt out of my element. As I observed a small group sharing jokes, their infectious laughter drew me in. I decided to approach them and cracked a light-hearted comment about the awkwardness of such gatherings. To my surprise, my quip sparked a wave of laughter, instantly dissolving my anxiety and allowing for a more genuine interaction. That moment taught me how humor could not only lighten the mood but also create a welcoming space for connection.

Creating an Inviting Atmosphere

Using humor to create an inviting atmosphere requires a blend of authenticity and attentiveness. The goal is to make others feel comfortable, valued, and included. Research from the *Journal of Personality and Social Psychology* emphasizes that individuals who exhibit warmth and humor are often perceived as more likable and approachable.

One of my favorite strategies involves observing the dynamics of a group before engaging. In a recent team meeting, I noticed that tensions were high as we discussed a challenging project. I made a conscious decision to lighten the mood by sharing a light-hearted story about a past project mishap, which evoked laughter and eased the group's anxiety. By creating an inviting atmosphere through humor, I facilitated a more open discussion where everyone felt empowered to share their ideas and concerns.

Timing is Everything

The effectiveness of humor often hinges on timing. Delivering a joke or witty remark at the right moment can transform the energy of a conversation. Research published in *Emotion* highlights that humor can defuse tense situations and improve interpersonal dynamics when used strategically.

In social situations, I've learned to be attentive to cues that signal when humor might be appropriate. For instance, during a conversation about stressful deadlines, I might interject with a humorous analogy, such as, "I feel like I'm racing against a tortoise on caffeine!" The laughter that follows not only lightens the mood but also opens the door for further discussion. Timing creates a shared moment of levity that fosters connection and camaraderie.

Finding Your Humor Style

Understanding your own humor style can help you connect with others more authentically. Humor can take various forms, such as self-deprecating, observational, or playful. Research from the *International Journal of Humor Research* indicates that people are generally drawn to those whose humor aligns with their own preferences.

Throughout my journey, I experimented with different styles of humor to discover what resonated most with me and those around me.

I found that self-deprecating humor often worked well for me, as it allowed me to disarm others and create relatability. For example, during a presentation, I once joked, "If my slides don't make sense, just pretend they're abstract art!" This approach not only eased my nerves but also invited the audience to engage with me more openly. Understanding my humor style helped me navigate social interactions with confidence.

Connecting Through Shared Laughter

Humor has a unique ability to create shared experiences that bond people together. When we laugh together, we foster a sense of belonging and connection. Research published in *Social Psychological and Personality Science* highlights that shared laughter can strengthen social bonds and increase feelings of closeness.

I noticed the impact of shared laughter during a family gathering. As we reminisced about funny moments from our past, laughter erupted around the table, creating an atmosphere of warmth and togetherness. It was a reminder that humor could bridge generational gaps and deepen familial connections. The shared experience of laughter not only reinforced our bonds but also created lasting memories that we could cherish.

Humor as a Stress Reliever

In high-pressure situations, humor can serve as an invaluable stress reliever. Research from the *Journal of Health Psychology* emphasizes that laughter can significantly reduce stress levels, making individuals feel more at ease in challenging circumstances.

I recall a particularly stressful day at work when a deadline loomed overhead. As my team grappled with tension, one colleague spontaneously imitated a famous movie character to lighten the mood. The laughter that followed served as a much-needed release, allowing us to approach our tasks with renewed energy. This experience reinforced my belief in the power of humor as a coping mechanism, reminding me that laughter can often be the best remedy in high-stress environments.

The Power of Playfulness

Playfulness is an integral part of effective humor. When we approach conversations with a sense of playfulness, we invite others to engage more openly. Research from *The Journal of Positive Psychology* highlights that playful interactions can enhance creativity and strengthen relationships.

I began to incorporate playful banter into my daily interactions. For example, when a coworker was struggling to meet a deadline, I playfully suggested they consider using a time machine to get ahead of their workload. This light-hearted comment not only broke the tension but also encouraged them to share their own struggles, creating a more supportive environment. Playfulness can transform even mundane conversations into engaging exchanges that foster connection.

Authenticity in Humor

Authenticity is crucial when using humor as a tool for connection. People can often sense when humor feels forced or inauthentic, which can undermine its effectiveness. Research published in *The Journal of Personality* emphasizes that individuals are drawn to those who exhibit genuine and relatable humor.

I made it a point to be authentic in my humor. Rather than trying to mimic others' comedic styles, I leaned into what felt natural for me. For example, when recounting a funny incident, I'd share my honest reaction rather than embellishing the story for effect. This authenticity not only resonated with my audience but also established a sense of trust. When humor feels genuine, it becomes a powerful connector, allowing for more meaningful interactions.

Embracing the Unexpected

Humor often thrives on the element of surprise. Unexpected twists in conversation can elicit laughter and create memorable moments. Research published in *Cognitive Psychology* indicates that surprise is a key component in what makes something funny, as it breaks established patterns of thought.

During a recent dinner party, I decided to embrace the unexpected by playfully critiquing my own cooking skills, saying, "If this meal turns out poorly, we'll call it a culinary experiment!" The laughter that followed not only lightened the atmosphere but also sparked a playful conversation about cooking mishaps, further enhancing the group's connection. Embracing the unexpected in humor can turn ordinary moments into shared experiences that foster intimacy.

Balancing Humor and Sensitivity

While humor can create an inviting atmosphere, it is essential to be mindful of the sensitivities of those around us. Understanding the context and the audience is critical for ensuring that humor enhances rather than detracts from a conversation. Research from *Communication Research* emphasizes the importance of context in humor, as missteps can lead to misunderstandings or hurt feelings.

I learned this lesson the hard way during a team-building event. Attempting to inject humor into a serious discussion about challenges, I made a joke that didn't land well. The room fell silent, and I quickly realized that the timing and context were off. From that experience, I became more attuned to the emotional climate of a situation, ensuring that my humor aligns with the feelings and experiences of others. Balancing humor with sensitivity allows for richer interactions that foster trust.

Using Humor to Build Rapport

Humor is an excellent tool for building rapport, especially in new or unfamiliar settings. When we share a laugh, we create a sense of familiarity and connection that breaks down barriers. Research from *The Journal of Social and Personal Relationships* highlights that humor can enhance interpersonal attraction and closeness.

I actively employed humor when meeting new colleagues or acquaintances. During an introductory meeting, I often began with a light-hearted comment about the common awkwardness of icebreakers. This approach not only made the atmosphere more relaxed but also invited others to share their own experiences, fostering a sense of camaraderie. Using humor as a bridge in new relationships paves the way for deeper connections.

Learning from Humor Failures

Not every attempt at humor will land successfully, and that's perfectly okay. Learning from humorous missteps can offer valuable insights into social dynamics and personal growth. Research published in *The Journal of Experimental Social Psychology* emphasizes that resilience in the face of humor failures can enhance social bonds.

I experienced this firsthand during a presentation when I attempted a joke that fell flat. Instead of retreating in embarrassment, I chose to laugh at my own expense, saying, "Well, that joke didn't work, but at least I tried!" The audience appreciated my vulnerability and the moment turned into a shared experience of laughter. Learning to embrace humor failures creates an atmosphere of acceptance and connection, allowing us to navigate social interactions more gracefully.

Expanding Your Humor Repertoire

To enhance your presence through humor, expanding your humor repertoire can be beneficial. Exploring different styles of humor, such as observational, situational, or absurd, can provide a variety of tools for connection. Research from *Psychological Bulletin* suggests that diverse humor styles can enrich interpersonal relationships.

I began to explore various sources of humor, from stand-up comedians to humorous literature. This exploration allowed me to identify what resonated with me and to practice incorporating different styles into my interactions. For example, I found that observational humor worked particularly well in casual conversations, as it allowed me to comment on shared experiences. Expanding your humor repertoire can enhance your ability to connect with a diverse range of individuals.

Humor as a Reflection of Values

The type of humor we embrace often reflects our values and worldview. Understanding how our humor aligns with our beliefs can create deeper connections with like-minded individuals. Research from *Personality and Individual Differences* highlights that shared values can enhance interpersonal attraction.

I noticed this connection during discussions with friends who shared similar values. Our shared sense of humor often centered around topics that mattered to us, such as social issues or personal growth. By engaging in humor that aligned with our values, we strengthened our bond and fostered meaningful conversations. Recognizing how humor reflects our values allows us to connect with others on a deeper level.

The Lasting Impact of Humor

Ultimately, the impact of humor extends beyond individual interactions; it has the potential to create lasting memories and connections. Shared laughter can transform a simple moment into an enduring bond that resonates through time. Research published in *Psychological Bulletin* emphasizes that positive shared experiences can enhance relationship satisfaction.

I experienced this when reflecting on a trip with friends. We spent hours laughing over shared mishaps and inside jokes, and those memories became touchstones in our friendship. Each recollection of laughter solidified our connection, creating a narrative that enriched our relationship. The lasting impact of humor serves as a reminder of the power of shared joy and its ability to enhance our connections with others.

Incorporating humor into our interactions not only enhances our presence but also fosters deeper connections and a sense of belonging. By understanding the dynamics of humor, practicing active engagement, and embracing authenticity, we can create inviting atmospheres that draw others in. As we navigate our social worlds, let us remember that laughter is a universal language that can bridge divides, foster intimacy, and enrich our relationships in ways we never imagined.

Personal Grooming and Style

When it comes to making a lasting impression, the importance of personal grooming and style cannot be overstated. How we present ourselves can significantly influence the way others perceive us, shaping interactions and relationships from the very first encounter. Through my own experiences and insights drawn from recent research, I've come to appreciate the nuanced role that grooming and style play in enhancing one's presence and attracting others effortlessly.

The Psychology of First Impressions

Research consistently shows that first impressions are formed within seconds of meeting someone. According to a study published in the *journal of Psychological Science*, it takes only a fraction of a second for people to form judgments about others based on appearance alone. These initial assessments can impact everything from job opportunities to personal relationships. With such significant stakes, understanding the psychology behind first impressions becomes crucial.

In my early career, I learned this lesson the hard way. I arrived at a crucial networking event feeling confident in my knowledge but decidedly underdressed. As I mingled with well-groomed colleagues, I couldn't shake the feeling that my appearance was overshadowing my expertise. This experience taught me that while skills and knowledge are vital, they can be overshadowed if we fail to pay attention to our presentation.

Grooming: The Basics Matter

Grooming encompasses the habits and practices that keep us looking and feeling our best. This includes everything from personal hygiene to hairstyle choices. According to a study published in *The Journal of Social Psychology*, well-groomed individuals are often perceived as more competent and trustworthy. This is particularly relevant in professional settings, where appearance can influence hiring decisions and promotions.

During my time in the corporate world, I made it a priority to establish a grooming routine that reflected my professional aspirations. Regular haircuts, maintaining clear skin, and practicing good hygiene became non-negotiables for me. I found that investing time in grooming not only enhanced my appearance but also boosted my confidence. The act of caring for myself became a ritual that set a positive tone for my day.

The Power of Clothing Choices

Clothing is an extension of our identity, and it communicates messages about who we are before we even say a word. Research published in *Fashion Theory* shows that clothing can influence how others perceive our personality traits, such as confidence and authority. The choices we make in our wardrobe can either enhance or detract from our presence.

I've experienced firsthand the impact of dressing appropriately for the occasion. On one occasion, I attended a casual gathering in a more formal outfit, and while I felt polished, I noticed that it created a distance between myself and the other attendees. They were dressed casually, and I seemed out of place. The experience underscored the importance of understanding the context of an event and dressing to match it. When I began to tailor my clothing choices to suit the occasion, I found it easier to connect with others.

Dressing for Success: The Professional Context

In a professional context, dressing for success involves more than just looking polished; it's about conveying confidence and competence. Studies indicate that attire can affect not only how others perceive us but also how we perceive ourselves. The phenomenon known as "enclothed cognition" suggests that the clothing we wear can influence our psychological states and behavior.

As I advanced in my career, I began to curate a wardrobe that reflected my aspirations. I learned to select clothing that not only fit well but also made me feel empowered. Tailored blazers, quality shoes, and well-fitted trousers became staples in my professional wardrobe. Each piece was chosen with intention, and I found that when I dressed confidently, my demeanor and interactions with others naturally followed suit.

Color Psychology and Personal Branding

The colors we choose to wear can evoke specific emotions and convey messages about our personalities. Research in color psychology highlights that different colors can influence perceptions and feelings. For instance, blue often conveys trust and dependability, while red can evoke passion and confidence.

In my quest to enhance my personal brand, I became more aware of how color choices affected my presence. I experimented with various colors to see how they influenced not only my mood but also how others responded to me. When I wore a deep navy suit, I noticed that colleagues were more likely to seek my input during meetings. Conversely, wearing bright colors elicited more playful interactions. Understanding the psychology of color helped me make more strategic choices in my wardrobe, allowing me to communicate effectively through my appearance.

Accessories: The Finishing Touch

Accessories are often the finishing touches that can elevate an outfit from ordinary to extraordinary. They offer an opportunity to express individuality and can enhance our overall appearance. Research published in the *Journal of Fashion Marketing and Management* suggests that well-chosen accessories can draw attention and enhance the perceived quality of an outfit.

I found that adding a few key accessories to my wardrobe made a significant difference in how I felt and how others perceived me. A classic watch or a unique tie could serve as conversation starters, inviting others to engage with me. Accessories also allowed me to express my personality, whether through a bold scarf or understated cufflinks. These small but impactful choices contributed to a more complete presentation of myself.

The Importance of Fit

One of the most critical aspects of personal grooming and style is the fit of our clothing. No matter how stylish an outfit may be, if it doesn't fit well, it can detract from our presence. Research indicates that well-fitting clothes can enhance our confidence and comfort levels, allowing us to engage more fully in social situations.

I discovered this lesson during my early attempts to find my professional style. Initially, I gravitated towards trendy clothing without paying attention to fit. However, after a wardrobe overhaul where I focused on tailored pieces, I realized the transformative power of fit. A well-fitted blazer or pair of trousers not only looked better but also allowed me to move with ease and confidence. This shift in focus on fit made a noticeable difference in how I carried myself and interacted with others.

Grooming Rituals: Building Confidence

Establishing grooming rituals can significantly impact our self-esteem and overall presence. Engaging in self-care routines not only enhances our appearance but also promotes a positive self-image. Research from *The Journal of Personal and Social Relationships* suggests that individuals who engage in self-care practices report higher levels of confidence and life satisfaction.

I made it a habit to carve out time for grooming rituals that made me feel good about myself. Whether it was a morning skincare routine, a fresh haircut, or simply taking time to choose an outfit I loved, these rituals became integral to my daily routine. I found that when I took the time to care for my appearance, it elevated my mood and allowed me to engage more authentically with others.

The Role of Body Language and Presence

While grooming and style are essential, body language plays a crucial role in enhancing our overall presence. How we carry ourselves can amplify or undermine our appearance. Research published in *Nonverbal Behavior* emphasizes that confident body language can enhance perceptions of competence and approachability.

I began to pay attention to my body language and how it interacted with my grooming and style. Standing tall, making eye contact, and offering a firm handshake became intentional practices. These nonverbal cues complemented my polished appearance and communicated confidence to those I interacted with. The combination of grooming, style, and confident body language created a powerful presence that attracted others effortlessly.

Adapting to Your Environment

Understanding the environment we are entering is key to presenting ourselves appropriately. Different settings—whether professional, casual, or social—require different approaches to grooming and style. Research from *Clothing and Textiles Research Journal* suggests that adapting our appearance to fit the context can enhance our comfort and confidence.

I learned to assess the environment before making grooming and style choices. For example, attending a business casual event called for a different approach than a formal conference. Being mindful of the context allowed me to feel comfortable and confident, enabling me to engage more effectively with others. Adapting to my surroundings reinforced my presence and made me more relatable.

The Cultural Dimensions of Style

Style is often influenced by cultural norms and expectations. Understanding these cultural dimensions can enhance our ability to connect with others and navigate social situations. Research in *International Journal of Cross-Cultural Management* highlights that being culturally aware can foster inclusivity and understanding.

I've found that my travels have opened my eyes to the diverse expressions of personal style across cultures. When visiting different countries, I took the opportunity to observe local fashion trends and grooming practices. This awareness allowed me to adapt my style while respecting cultural norms. It became a way to connect with individuals from various backgrounds, demonstrating my appreciation for their culture while expressing my own.

Developing a Personal Style

Cultivating a personal style is an ongoing journey that reflects our evolving identities. Personal style is not just about following trends; it's about finding what resonates with us and expressing it authentically. Research from *Fashion and Textiles* suggests that individuals who embrace their personal style report higher levels of self-esteem and self-acceptance.

As I navigated my style journey, I focused on identifying pieces that truly resonated with me. I experimented with various combinations, observing what made me feel confident and authentic. Over time, I curated a wardrobe that reflected my personality and values. This process of self-discovery not only enhanced my appearance but also allowed me to engage with others more authentically.

Building a Supportive Network

Surrounding ourselves with individuals who value grooming and style can positively impact our own habits and self-perception. Research from *The Journal of Social Psychology* highlights the influence of social networks on personal grooming practices.

I noticed that the people I spent time with often influenced my own grooming and style choices. Friends who prioritized personal care inspired me to do the same. Engaging in discussions about fashion, grooming tips, and self-care rituals created a supportive environment that encouraged us all to elevate our presence. Building a network that values grooming and style can serve as a powerful motivator for personal growth.

The Impact of Social Media

In today's digital age, social media plays a significant role in shaping perceptions of grooming and style. Platforms like Instagram and

Pinterest serve as visual inspiration, showcasing diverse styles and grooming practices. However, it's essential to approach social media with a discerning eye, as curated images can create unrealistic standards.

I learned to leverage social media as a source of inspiration rather than comparison. By following accounts that aligned with my personal style and values, I gained new ideas while remaining true to myself. I also made a conscious effort to engage with my own social media presence, sharing authentic moments that reflected my journey in grooming and style. This balance allowed me to navigate the digital landscape while enhancing my real-world presence.

A Holistic Approach to Presence

Ultimately, enhancing your presence through personal grooming and style involves a holistic approach. It encompasses not only appearance but also confidence, body language, and social awareness. Research consistently supports the idea that a well-rounded approach to personal presentation leads to more positive social interactions.

As I reflected on my journey, I realized that the most magnetic individuals I encountered embodied a combination of grooming, style, and genuine confidence. They exuded an energy that drew people in, making them approachable and relatable. By embracing a holistic approach to my presence, I found that I could attract others effortlessly while fostering deeper connections.

Focusing on personal grooming and style is not just about outward appearance; it's about creating a positive self-image and embodying the confidence that attracts others. By investing in our grooming habits, making intentional clothing choices, and cultivating an authentic personal style, we can enhance our presence and connect more meaningfully with those around us. In a world where first impressions matter, the journey toward personal grooming and style becomes an essential part of attracting others effortlessly.

Chapter 6: Cultivating a Magnetic Lifestyle Passion and Purpose

Living a life infused with passion and purpose is one of the most compelling ways to attract others. When you engage others through your interests and goals, you create a magnetic aura that draws people in, inviting them to share in your journey. This isn't merely about superficial charm; it's about embodying a vibrant, authentic energy that resonates with those around you. My own experiences, combined with insights from recent research, reveal how cultivating a lifestyle centered on passion and purpose can transform both your life and the lives of those you connect with.

• • • •

THE POWER OF PASSION

Passion is an intense enthusiasm for something that fuels your energy and inspires action. It's infectious. When you speak about what excites you, that enthusiasm translates into a compelling narrative that others want to be part of. Research in *Psychology Today* has shown that passionate people are often perceived as more attractive and charismatic. They naturally draw others toward them because they seem alive and engaged.

Reflecting on my journey, I remember a period when I felt unfulfilled in my routine job. It wasn't until I rekindled my passion for writing and storytelling that I noticed a shift in how others responded to me. Engaging with fellow writers, sharing my experiences, and discussing literature sparked conversations that were richer and more meaningful. My excitement became a conduit for connection, allowing others to see not just my interests but also the depth of my character.

Finding Your Passion

Identifying what you are truly passionate about can take time and reflection. Many people feel pressure to follow predefined paths, often losing sight of what genuinely excites them. Research from *The Journal of Positive Psychology* emphasizes the importance of pursuing passions that align with personal values for overall life satisfaction.

To discover my passions, I engaged in a process of exploration. I took classes, attended workshops, and even volunteered in areas that piqued my interest. Each experience provided clarity, helping me identify what resonated with my core values. I encourage readers to embark on their own exploration. Keep a journal of activities that ignite a spark in you, and allow yourself the freedom to pursue them without judgment.

Purpose: The Driving Force

While passion energizes us, purpose gives our lives direction. It's the underlying reason for why we do what we do, shaping our goals and guiding our decisions. According to research from *Harvard Business Review*, people who have a clear sense of purpose not only experience greater satisfaction in life but are also perceived as more attractive to others.

I discovered my purpose through introspection and dialogue with mentors and friends. I realized that my love for storytelling was not just about writing; it was about connecting with others and sharing experiences. This revelation allowed me to align my professional goals with my passion for communication, creating a powerful synergy that enhanced my presence in social situations.

To identify your purpose, consider what legacy you want to leave behind. What impact do you want to have on your community or the world? Reflecting on these questions can help clarify your motivations and align your actions with your values.

Engaging Others Through Your Interests

Once you've identified your passions and purpose, the next step is to engage others through these interests. People are naturally drawn to those who have a clear sense of what they love. Sharing your passions can create common ground, fostering connections that go beyond surface-level interactions.

I learned this lesson when I joined a local book club. As I shared my thoughts on various works of literature, I discovered how much people appreciated hearing about my perspectives and insights. The conversations flowed easily, and I was able to connect with fellow members on a deeper level. This experience reinforced the idea that when you share your interests genuinely, you invite others to join you on that journey.

Building Community Around Shared Interests

Creating a community around your passions can amplify their magnetic effect. Engaging in activities that connect you with like-minded individuals not only enriches your experience but also expands your network. Research from *Social Networks* indicates that shared interests are a strong predictor of relationship formation.

I took the initiative to organize workshops and events centered around writing and storytelling. Inviting others to share their stories and insights cultivated an environment where we could learn from each other. These gatherings turned into regular meetups, and friendships blossomed from the shared enthusiasm. By nurturing a community, I found that the collective passion created a vibrant atmosphere that attracted even more individuals.

Leveraging Social Media

In our digital age, social media offers an unparalleled platform for sharing your passions and engaging with others. It's a powerful tool for connecting with people who share similar interests, no matter where they are in the world. Research published in *Computers in Human Behavior* highlights that social media can foster social connections and deepen relationships through shared experiences.

I began to leverage platforms like Instagram and Twitter to share my writing journey. Posting snippets of my work, engaging in discussions, and connecting with other writers created a sense of community that extended beyond physical boundaries. The feedback and support I received enriched my passion and inspired me to keep pushing forward. By authentically sharing my interests, I found myself forming connections with individuals who resonated with my journey.

Cultivating Curiosity

Curiosity is an essential component of a magnetic lifestyle. When you approach life with a sense of wonder, you're more likely to engage with others in meaningful ways. Research from *Personality and Social Psychology Bulletin* indicates that curious individuals are perceived as more attractive because they're often open to new experiences and ideas.

I cultivated my curiosity by asking questions and actively listening to others. When engaging in conversations, I made a conscious effort to explore others' interests and perspectives. This not only deepened my connections but also created a dynamic exchange where people felt valued and understood. Curiosity fosters an inviting atmosphere, making it easier to connect with a diverse range of individuals.

Setting Goals and Sharing Your Journey

Setting goals aligned with your passions and purpose can create a compelling narrative that attracts others. When you share your journey toward achieving these goals, you invite others to join you in your pursuit. Research published in *Journal of Applied Psychology* emphasizes that people are inspired by those who are working toward meaningful objectives.

I began to set personal and professional goals related to my writing. By sharing my progress on social media and during community events, I not only held myself accountable but also inspired others to pursue their aspirations. The support I received from my network reinforced my motivation, creating a positive feedback loop that further fueled my passion.

Overcoming Obstacles Together

Life is filled with challenges, and sharing these obstacles can create deeper connections with others. Vulnerability fosters authenticity, allowing people to see the real you. Research from *Brené Brown* emphasizes that embracing vulnerability strengthens relationships and enhances connection.

I've encountered my share of setbacks in my creative pursuits, from writer's block to rejection. When I opened up about these struggles during conversations, I found that others were eager to share their own experiences. This exchange created a sense of camaraderie, reinforcing our bonds. By embracing vulnerability, we not only create deeper connections but also foster an environment where others feel safe to share their journeys.

The Ripple Effect of Passion and Purpose

Living with passion and purpose doesn't just benefit you; it creates a ripple effect that influences those around you. When you engage others through your interests, you inspire them to explore their own passions and pursue their purposes. Research from *The Journal of Positive Psychology* indicates that individuals who witness others pursuing their passions are more likely to feel motivated to do the same.

I observed this phenomenon firsthand during one of my writing workshops. As participants shared their stories and goals, I noticed a shift in the room. People who had initially seemed reserved began to express their excitement and aspirations. This collective enthusiasm created an environment charged with creativity, inspiring everyone to embrace their passions more fully.

Embracing Change and Growth

A magnetic lifestyle is not static; it evolves as we grow and change. Embracing new experiences and remaining open to change allows us to continue engaging others in meaningful ways. Research from *The Journal of Personality and Social Psychology* underscores the importance of adaptability in sustaining relationships.

I've found that being open to new passions has enriched my life in unexpected ways. Whether it's exploring new writing genres or attending workshops outside my comfort zone, each experience has added depth to my journey. Sharing these experiences with others not only keeps my narrative fresh but also invites them to explore their own potential for growth.

The Art of Attracting Through Passion

Living a magnetic lifestyle rooted in passion and purpose is a powerful way to attract others effortlessly. Engaging with those around you through your interests and goals creates a vibrant tapestry of connections that enrich your life and theirs. By fostering a community, sharing your journey, and embracing curiosity, you create an inviting atmosphere where deeper relationships can flourish.

As you embark on this journey, remember that authenticity is key. When you align your passions with your purpose and share them genuinely, you not only enhance your presence but also invite others to join you on a remarkable adventure. Embrace your interests, pursue your goals, and watch as the world becomes a more connected and engaging place, one relationship at a time.

Expanding Your Social Circle

Expanding your social circle is a fundamental aspect of cultivating a magnetic lifestyle. Engaging with new people not only enriches your experiences but also opens doors to opportunities you may never have anticipated. Through my personal journey and insights from recent research, I've learned effective techniques for meeting new people and building networks that can enhance both your personal and professional life.

The Mindset of Connection

The first step to expanding your social circle is adopting a mindset geared toward connection. When you approach new social situations with curiosity and openness, you create an inviting atmosphere that encourages others to engage with you. Research in *Social Psychology* emphasizes that a positive mindset can significantly influence social interactions, making you appear more approachable and friendly.

I remember a time when I was apprehensive about networking events. My nerves often held me back from striking up conversations. However, I gradually shifted my perspective. Instead of viewing these gatherings as opportunities to "sell" myself, I began to see them as chances to learn about others and form connections. This mindset change transformed my interactions, allowing me to engage more naturally and confidently.

Setting Clear Intentions

Being clear about what you want to achieve can also guide your efforts in expanding your social circle. Whether you seek professional connections, friendships, or mentorship, defining your intentions can shape your approach and interactions. Research from *The Journal of Applied Psychology* suggests that having clear goals enhances motivation and focus, leading to better outcomes.

I started to set intentions before attending events or social gatherings. For instance, if I aimed to meet three new people or gather insights on a specific topic, I would keep those goals in mind throughout the event. This focus not only helped me stay motivated but also made my interactions more purposeful. As I engaged in conversations, I found it easier to steer discussions toward my intentions, resulting in deeper and more meaningful connections.

••••

LEVERAGING EXISTING Networks

Expanding your social circle doesn't always mean starting from scratch. Often, your existing network can be a valuable resource for meeting new people. Research in *Sociological Review* highlights that weak ties—connections you may not know well—can serve as bridges to new social circles.

I found that reaching out to acquaintances for introductions led to unexpected opportunities. For instance, I once asked a friend to introduce me to her colleague, who shared my interest in writing. That introduction blossomed into a collaborative project that significantly enhanced my professional network. By leveraging existing relationships, you can efficiently expand your reach and create meaningful connections.

Attending Events and Workshops

Participating in events and workshops related to your interests is one of the most effective ways to meet new people. These settings provide a natural environment for interaction and connection. Research published in *Journal of Community & Applied Social Psychology* indicates that individuals are more likely to bond over shared interests, creating a foundation for lasting relationships.

I made a habit of attending local workshops, seminars, and networking events in my field. Each event was an opportunity to learn and connect with like-minded individuals. I remember one particular writing workshop where we not only honed our skills but also exchanged ideas and contact information. This experience solidified friendships that have enriched both my personal and professional life.

Utilizing Online Platforms

In the digital age, online platforms can be powerful tools for expanding your social circle. Social media, networking sites, and online forums provide avenues for connecting with individuals who share your interests. Research in *Computers in Human Behavior* underscores that online interactions can lead to offline relationships, enhancing social capital.

I began exploring platforms like LinkedIn, Meetup, and even Facebook groups centered around writing and creativity. Participating in discussions, attending virtual events, and joining local meetups expanded my network significantly. I learned to approach these platforms with authenticity, sharing my interests and seeking genuine connections. This strategy allowed me to form meaningful relationships that often translated into real-world interactions.

Mastering the Art of Small Talk

Small talk is a crucial skill in meeting new people. While it may seem trivial, mastering this art can facilitate deeper conversations and connections. Research in *Communication Research* highlights that effective small talk can lead to more substantial interactions, helping to establish rapport and trust.

I practiced small talk by engaging in casual conversations wherever I went—at coffee shops, during commutes, or in social settings. I focused on open-ended questions that invited others to share their experiences. Instead of asking, "Did you have a good weekend?" I would say, "What did you do over the weekend?" This shift often opened doors to more engaging discussions. Over time, I became more comfortable initiating conversations, which enhanced my ability to connect with new people.

Active Listening as a Connection Tool

Active listening is an essential component of effective communication. It fosters genuine connections and demonstrates that you value others' perspectives. Research in *International Journal of Listening* indicates that active listeners are perceived as more empathetic and approachable.

I learned the importance of active listening during my interactions. Instead of simply waiting for my turn to speak, I focused on truly understanding the other person's message. Nodding, maintaining eye contact, and summarizing what they said helped me engage more meaningfully. By creating an atmosphere of openness, I found that people were more inclined to share their stories and insights, which deepened our connection.

Being Authentic and Vulnerable

Authenticity is a magnet for connection. When you present your true self, people are drawn to your genuine nature. Vulnerability, while sometimes daunting, can also foster deeper relationships. Research from *Brené Brown* emphasizes that vulnerability is key to building trust and connection.

I discovered that sharing my challenges and aspirations made me more relatable. During conversations, I would openly discuss my struggles with writing or the fears I faced in pursuing my passion. This authenticity encouraged others to reciprocate, leading to more profound and meaningful exchanges. When people feel safe to be vulnerable, connections deepen, and relationships flourish.

Finding Common Ground

Identifying common interests can significantly enhance your ability to connect with others. Research published in *Social Networks* suggests that shared experiences and interests form the basis of strong relationships. When you find common ground, you create a sense of belonging that draws people closer.

During social gatherings, I made a conscious effort to ask questions that revealed shared interests. For instance, asking about favorite books or hobbies often led to lively discussions. I remember bonding with a new acquaintance over our mutual love for a specific genre of literature, which sparked further conversations and ultimately, a lasting friendship. By seeking common ground, you create a natural foundation for building connections.

Nurturing Relationships

Expanding your social circle is not just about making new connections; it's also about nurturing those relationships over time. Regular follow-ups and maintaining contact can solidify bonds and ensure that connections remain vibrant. Research in *Journal of Social and Personal Relationships* underscores the importance of ongoing engagement in sustaining relationships.

I made it a point to check in with new acquaintances after initial meetings. Sending a quick message to say I enjoyed our conversation or sharing an article related to our discussion kept the connection alive. Additionally, I organized casual meetups or coffee catch-ups to deepen these relationships. By investing time and effort into nurturing connections, I found that my social circle naturally expanded and enriched my life.

Embracing Diversity

Diversity in your social circle can enhance your perspectives and experiences. Engaging with individuals from different backgrounds, cultures, and fields broadens your horizons and fosters personal growth. Research from *Cultural Diversity and Ethnic Minority Psychology* highlights that diverse social networks can improve creativity and problem-solving.

I intentionally sought to diversify my social circle by attending events that attracted people from various backgrounds. Engaging in conversations with individuals who had different life experiences often led to enriching discussions. For instance, a conversation with someone from a different cultural background opened my eyes to new ways of thinking about storytelling. Embracing diversity not only enriched my social circle but also expanded my understanding of the world.

Volunteering and Community Involvement

Engaging in volunteer work or community activities is a powerful way to meet new people while contributing to a cause you care about. Research published in *Nonprofit and Voluntary Sector Quarterly* indicates that volunteering fosters social connections and can lead to long-lasting friendships.

I began volunteering at a local nonprofit focused on literacy and education. This experience allowed me to meet passionate individuals who shared my values. Working alongside others toward a common goal fostered a sense of camaraderie and purpose. The relationships formed in this environment were often deeper and more meaningful because they were built on shared values and experiences.

Being Open to New Experiences

Being open to new experiences can create unexpected opportunities for connection. When you step outside your comfort zone, you not only expand your horizons but also increase your chances of meeting new people. Research from *Personality and Social Psychology Bulletin* suggests that openness to experience is linked to social engagement and relationship-building.

I challenged myself to try new activities, from attending dance classes to joining local hiking groups. Each new experience brought me into contact with individuals I might never have met otherwise. I remember striking up a conversation with a fellow participant during a pottery class, which eventually led to a friendship centered around our mutual interest in creativity. Embracing new experiences has been instrumental in expanding my social circle and fostering connections.

The Importance of Follow-Up

After meeting someone new, the follow-up is crucial in solidifying connections. A simple message expressing your enjoyment of the conversation can leave a lasting impression. Research in *Journal of*

Social and Personal Relationships highlights that timely follow-ups can enhance relationship satisfaction and longevity.

I made it a habit to follow up with new acquaintances within a few days of meeting. Whether through email or social media, a brief note expressing my appreciation for our conversation often prompted further interaction. This practice not only reinforced our connection but also opened the door for future meetups or collaborations.

Creating a Personal Brand

Your personal brand plays a vital role in attracting the right people into your social circle. By intentionally cultivating your image and online presence, you can draw individuals who resonate with your values and interests. Research from *Harvard Business Review* indicates that a strong personal brand enhances visibility and opportunities.

I worked on developing my personal brand by curating my online profiles to reflect my passions and professional aspirations. Sharing content related to writing and storytelling not only showcased my interests but also attracted like-minded individuals. By being intentional about my personal brand, I found that I naturally connected with those who shared similar values, enriching my social circle.

Celebrating Your Connections

Celebrating milestones and achievements, whether big or small, can reinforce your connections with others. Acknowledging the successes of friends and acquaintances fosters a sense of community and support. Research in *Journal of Personality and Social Psychology* underscores the importance of celebrating together in strengthening relationships.

I made it a practice to celebrate the achievements of those in my social circle. Whether it was attending a friend's book launch or simply sending a congratulatory message, these gestures deepened our bonds. By actively celebrating each other's successes, we created a supportive environment where everyone felt valued and appreciated.

Adapting to Change

As you expand your social circle, it's essential to recognize that relationships may evolve over time. People grow, interests change, and priorities shift. Being adaptable and open to these changes can help you maintain connections while also allowing for new ones to form. Research from *Personal Relationships* suggests that adaptability is a key factor in sustaining long-term relationships.

I learned to embrace change within my social circle by being open to new dynamics. Friendships that once revolved around specific interests may evolve as lives change, and that's perfectly natural. By remaining adaptable and receptive to these shifts, I found that I could maintain meaningful connections while also welcoming new relationships into my life.

Investing in Your Network

Investing time and effort into your social circle is crucial for building and maintaining connections. Regularly engaging with others, whether through meetups, phone calls, or online interactions, keeps relationships vibrant. Research in *Social Network Analysis* emphasizes that consistent investment in relationships leads to stronger social ties.

I made it a priority to regularly connect with friends and acquaintances. I scheduled coffee catch-ups, organized group outings, and reached out just to check in. This investment of time demonstrated my commitment to nurturing those relationships, leading to a more robust and interconnected social circle.

The Journey of Connection

Expanding your social circle is a dynamic and ongoing journey. By adopting a mindset geared toward connection, setting clear intentions, and actively engaging with others, you can create a vibrant network that enriches your life. Through shared experiences, authenticity, and openness to new opportunities, you'll find that the art of attracting others effortlessly becomes a natural part of your life.

As you embark on this journey, remember that every interaction holds the potential for connection. Embrace the process, celebrate the relationships you build, and continue to cultivate a magnetic lifestyle that invites new people into your life.

Conclusion: The Journey of Attraction

Reflecting on your growth in the realm of attraction requires recognizing that personal development is not a destination but a lifelong journey. Throughout this exploration, you've learned that the ability to attract others effortlessly stems from a deep understanding of yourself and the relationships you cultivate. This ongoing process shapes not only how you connect with others but also how you view yourself in the world.

The Ongoing Nature of Personal Development

Personal growth is an ever-evolving journey. It's easy to think of attraction as a static skill—something that can be mastered and then set aside. However, the truth is far more nuanced. Attraction encompasses a range of interpersonal skills, emotional intelligence, and self-awareness that adapt as we encounter new experiences and meet diverse people.

In my own journey, I've noticed that every new connection offers insights into my strengths and areas for improvement. For example, after a particularly engaging conversation with a stranger at a networking event, I realized that my active listening skills had improved. Yet, I also recognized moments where I could have shared more of my own experiences. This reflection drove me to delve deeper into understanding what makes conversations meaningful. Research in *Positive Psychology* supports this idea, emphasizing that continuous reflection fosters greater self-awareness, which in turn enhances interpersonal relationships.

As you continue to attract others into your life, reflect regularly on your experiences. Consider journaling about your interactions or discussing your thoughts with trusted friends. This practice not only helps solidify your learning but also enables you to identify patterns in your behavior and interactions. What worked well? What felt awkward? These reflections will guide your future interactions and refine your approach to building relationships.

• • • •

EMBRACING VULNERABILITY

Vulnerability is another crucial component of personal development. While it can be intimidating to share your true self with others, this authenticity creates deeper connections. My experiences have taught me that moments of vulnerability often lead to the most meaningful conversations. When I allowed myself to be open about my fears or aspirations, I noticed that others were more willing to reciprocate.

Brené Brown's research on vulnerability shows that it fosters trust and connection. When you share your authentic self, you invite others to do the same, creating an atmosphere of mutual understanding. Practicing vulnerability in safe spaces, such as close friendships or supportive communities, can help you build the confidence to bring this openness into new social settings.

Cultivating Emotional Intelligence

Emotional intelligence is another vital aspect of attracting others. It involves recognizing and responding to your own emotions and those of others. As you grow in this area, you'll find that your ability to connect with people deepens.

Throughout my journey, I learned to tune into the emotions of those around me. By observing body language and listening actively, I could gauge how others were feeling and adjust my responses accordingly. For instance, during a conversation with a colleague who seemed overwhelmed, I chose to listen without offering immediate solutions, allowing them the space to express their feelings. This small shift not only strengthened our rapport but also demonstrated the power of empathy in connection.

Research in *Emotional Intelligence* highlights that individuals with high emotional intelligence are more adept at forming and maintaining relationships. As you work on this skill, practice recognizing your emotional responses and those of others. Journaling about your interactions can help you process these emotions and develop strategies for more effective communication.

Taking Action: Practical Steps for Implementation

With a foundation of self-reflection and emotional intelligence, the next step is to take action. Implementing your newfound skills in daily life requires intention and practice. Consider the following practical steps to enhance your ability to attract others effortlessly.

Set Daily Intentions: Each day, take a moment to set an intention related to your social interactions. This could be as simple as "I will engage one new person today" or "I will listen actively during conversations." By clarifying your goals, you'll create a sense of purpose that guides your actions.

Practice Small Talk: Small talk serves as a gateway to deeper conversations. Challenge yourself to initiate small talk in various settings—while waiting in line, at coffee shops, or during social gatherings. The more you practice, the more comfortable you will become.

Host Gatherings: Create opportunities for connection by hosting gatherings, whether it's a dinner party, game night, or casual meetup. This not only allows you to showcase your interests but also fosters a welcoming environment for others to connect.

Expand Your Horizons: Make it a goal to step outside your comfort zone regularly. Attend events, join clubs, or take classes that interest you. Engaging in new activities not only enriches your life but also introduces you to potential connections.

Follow Up: After meeting someone new, make it a practice to follow up within a few days. A simple message expressing your enjoyment of the conversation or suggesting a coffee catch-up can solidify the connection and lay the groundwork for future interactions.

Engage in Active Listening: In every conversation, focus on being fully present. Put away distractions and maintain eye contact. Nod and respond appropriately to show that you value the other person's input. This small effort can significantly enhance the quality of your interactions.

Seek Feedback: Don't hesitate to ask trusted friends for feedback on your social interactions. They can provide valuable insights into your strengths and areas for growth, helping you refine your approach to connecting with others.

Reflect on Experiences: After social events, take time to reflect on your experiences. Consider what went well and what could be improved. This reflection can guide your future interactions and help you adapt your approach over time.

Volunteer: Engage in community service or volunteer work. This not only allows you to meet new people but also creates a shared purpose that can enhance connections.

Celebrate Your Progress: Acknowledge your growth and the connections you've made. Whether it's a small win or a significant milestone, celebrating these moments can reinforce your motivation to continue building relationships.

The Power of Authenticity

As you implement these steps, remember that authenticity is your greatest asset. People are drawn to genuine connections, and when you present your true self, you naturally attract others who resonate with your values and interests.

Reflecting on my journey, I recall how freeing it felt to embrace my authentic self. Initially, I worried about what others would think, but over time, I realized that authenticity was the key to forming meaningful relationships. The connections I formed by being true to myself have proven to be the most rewarding.

Staying Open to Growth

As you embark on this journey of attraction, remain open to learning and evolving. Each interaction offers a chance to grow, and every relationship contributes to your understanding of yourself and others. Embrace the idea that attraction is not just about making connections but about cultivating a rich tapestry of relationships that enrich your life.

Remember that everyone you meet has a story to tell, and your willingness to engage, listen, and connect can make a profound difference in their lives and yours. Be curious, stay humble, and approach each interaction with an open heart and mind.

As you continue to develop your skills, remember that the art of attraction is about more than just attracting others. It's about creating a fulfilling, connected life that celebrates the beauty of relationships in all their forms. This journey will not only enhance your ability to attract others effortlessly but also transform the way you experience life and connection.

By embracing growth, taking action, and remaining authentic, you will find that attracting others becomes a natural extension of who you are. With each new connection, you expand your world and create a vibrant network that reflects the richness of your journey.

Don't miss out!

Visit the website below and you can sign up to receive emails whenever Jason Lorayne publishes a new book. There's no charge and no obligation.

https://books2read.com/r/B-A-PYWSC-UVZGF

BOOKS 2 READ

Connecting independent readers to independent writers.

Milton Keynes UK
Ingram Content Group UK Ltd.
UKHW021919231124
451423UK00015B/199